OPPOSING VIEWPOINTS® SERIES



# The Corporatization of America

# Other Books of Related Interest

## Opposing Viewpoints Series

America's Infrastructure and the Green Economy
Government Gridlock
White Collar Crime

## At Issue Series

Partisanship
The Politicization of the Supreme Court
The Media's Influence on Society

## Current Controversies Series

America's Role in a Changing World
Big Tech and Democracy
The Capitol Riot: Fragile Democracy

> "Congress shall make no law … abridging the freedom of speech, or of the press."
>
> *First Amendment to the U.S. Constitution*

The basic foundation of our democracy is the First Amendment guarantee of freedom of expression. The Opposing Viewpoints series is dedicated to the concept of this basic freedom and the idea that it is more important to practice it than to enshrine it.

OPPOSING VIEWPOINTS® SERIES

# The Corporatization of America

Avery Elizabeth Hurt, Book Editor

GREENHAVEN PUBLISHING

Published in 2023 by Greenhaven Publishing, LLC
2544 Clinton Street,
Buffalo NY 14224



First Edition



Articles in Greenhaven Publishing anthologies are often edited for length to meet page requirements. In addition, original titles of these works are changed to clearly present the main thesis and to explicitly indicate the author's opinion. Every effort is made to ensure that Greenhaven Publishing accurately reflects the original intent of the authors. Every effort has been made to trace the owners of the copyrighted material.

Cover image: New Africa/Shutterstock.com

**Library of Congress CataloginginPublication Data**

Names: Hurt, Avery Elizabeth, editor.
Title: The corporatization of America / Avery Elizabeth Hurt, book editor.
Description: First edition. | New York : Greenhaven Publishing, 2023. | Series: Opposing viewpoints | Includes bibliographical references and index. | Audience: Ages 15+ | Audience: Grades 10-12
Identifiers: LCCN 2022047781 | ISBN 9781534509245 (library binding) | ISBN 9781534509238 (paperback)
Subjects: LCSH: Corporations--United States--Juvenile literature.
Classification: LCC HD2785 .C596 2023 | DDC 338.7/40973--dc23/eng/20230119
LC record available at https://lccn.loc.gov/2022047781

*Manufactured in the United States of America*

Website: http://greenhavenpublishing.com

# Contents

**The Importance of Opposing Viewpoints** **11**

**Introduction** **14**

## Chapter 1: Do Corporations Have Too Much Power?

**Chapter Preface** 18

1. Today's Companies Need to Focus on Long-Term Values 19
   *Marc Goedhart and Tim Koller*
2. Corporations Can Be a Force for Good in Fighting Climate Change 28
   *Matt Gitsham, Ajit Nayak, and Jonathan Gosling*
3. Emphasis on Short-Term Profits Is Incompatible with Addressing Climate Change 34
   *Christopher Wright and Daniel Nyberg*
4. To Truly Do Good, Businesses Need to Overhaul Their Business Models and Corporate Cultures 39
   *Nishant Bagadia*

**Periodical and Internet Sources Bibliography** 45

## Chapter 2: Is Corporate Power a Danger to Democracy?

**Chapter Preface** 48

1. For Public Media to Serve the Public, It Must Get More Government Funding 49
   *Christopher Chávez*
2. Corporate and Government Control of Media Stifles Democracy and Crushes Dissent 55
   *Data Leads*
3. Democracy Is Good for Business 62
   *Sarah Repucci*
4. Corporations Have Too Much Power, Americans Say 67
   *Pew Research Center*

5. More Funding for Public Media Would Help, but Not Enough to Heal America's Political Divide 77
*Joshua Benton*

6. Repairing Media Could Help Repair Democracy 86
*Alina Ladyzhensky*

**Periodical and Internet Sources Bibliography** 91


## Chapter 3: Does Corporate Influence Taint Medicine and Scientific Research?


**Chapter Preface** 94

1. The Drug Industry Manipulates Scientific Research 95
*Richard Harris*

2. Corporate Corruption of Medical Science Is Deeper than Just Funding 99
*Sergio Sismondo*

3. The Public Doesn't Trust Scientific Research When Companies Are Involved 111
*John C. Besley, Aaron M. McCright, Joseph D. Martin, Kevin Elliot, and Nagwan Zahry*

4. When Health Care Is a Business, Patients Can Suffer at the Expense of Revenue 116
*Teodora Elena Ucenic*

5. Health Care Markets Need Just the Right Amount of Regulation 123
*Stuart Guterman*

**Periodical and Internet Sources Bibliography** 129


## Chapter 4: Do Tech Companies Have Too Much Power?


**Chapter Preface** 132

1. Americans Shouldn't Be Dependent on the Generosity of the Wealthy, but the Need for Big Philanthropy Is Here to Stay 133
*David Callahan*

2. Fake News Endangers Democracy 140
*Center for Information Technology and Society*
3. Americans Who Get News Mainly on Social Media Are Less Knowledgeable and Less Engaged 150
*Tom Infield*
4. Banning Users Is Not a Violation of the First Amendment by Big Tech 155
*Jennifer Huddleston*
**Periodical and Internet Sources Bibliography** 162

**For Further Discussion** 164
**Organizations to Contact** **167**
**Bibliography of Books** **171**
**Index** **173**

# The Importance of Opposing Viewpoints

Perhaps every generation experiences a period in time in which the populace seems especially polarized, starkly divided on the important issues of the day and gravitating toward the far ends of the political spectrum and away from a consensus-facilitating middle ground. The world that today's students are growing up in and that they will soon enter into as active and engaged citizens is deeply fragmented in just this way. Issues relating to terrorism, immigration, women's rights, minority rights, race relations, health care, taxation, wealth and poverty, the environment, policing, military intervention, the proper role of government—in some ways, perennial issues that are freshly and uniquely urgent and vital with each new generation—are currently roiling the world.

If we are to foster a knowledgeable, responsible, active, and engaged citizenry among today's youth, we must provide them with the intellectual, interpretive, and critical-thinking tools and experience necessary to make sense of the world around them and of the all-important debates and arguments that inform it. After all, the outcome of these debates will in large measure determine the future course, prospects, and outcomes of the world and its peoples, particularly its youth. If they are to become successful members of society and productive and informed citizens, students need to learn how to evaluate the strengths and weaknesses of someone else's arguments, how to sift fact from opinion and fallacy, and how to test the relative merits and validity of their own opinions against the known facts and the best possible available information. The landmark series Opposing Viewpoints has been providing students with just such critical-thinking skills and exposure to the debates surrounding society's most urgent contemporary issues for many years, and it continues to serve this essential role with undiminished commitment, care, and rigor.

The key to the series's success in achieving its goal of sharpening students' critical-thinking and analytic skills resides in its title—

Opposing Viewpoints. In every intriguing, compelling, and engaging volume of this series, readers are presented with the widest possible spectrum of distinct viewpoints, expert opinions, and informed argumentation and commentary, supplied by some of today's leading academics, thinkers, analysts, politicians, policy makers, economists, activists, change agents, and advocates. Every opinion and argument anthologized here is presented objectively and accorded respect. There is no editorializing in any introductory text or in the arrangement and order of the pieces. No piece is included as a "straw man," an easy ideological target for cheap point-scoring. As wide and inclusive a range of viewpoints as possible is offered, with no privileging of one particular political ideology or cultural perspective over another. It is left to each individual reader to evaluate the relative merits of each argument—as he or she sees it, and with the use of ever-growing critical-thinking skills—and grapple with his or her own assumptions, beliefs, and perspectives to determine how convincing or successful any given argument is and how the reader's own stance on the issue may be modified or altered in response to it.

This process is facilitated and supported by volume, chapter, and selection introductions that provide readers with the essential context they need to begin engaging with the spotlighted issues, with the debates surrounding them, and with their own perhaps shifting or nascent opinions on them. In addition, guided reading and discussion questions encourage readers to determine the authors' point of view and purpose, interrogate and analyze the various arguments and their rhetoric and structure, evaluate the arguments' strengths and weaknesses, test their claims against available facts and evidence, judge the validity of the reasoning, and bring into clearer, sharper focus the reader's own beliefs and conclusions and how they may differ from or align with those in the collection or those of their classmates.

Research has shown that reading comprehension skills improve dramatically when students are provided with compelling, intriguing, and relevant "discussable" texts. The subject matter of these collections could not be more compelling, intriguing, or urgently relevant to today's students and the world they are poised to inherit. The anthologized articles and the reading and discussion questions that are included with them also provide the basis for stimulating, lively, and passionate classroom debates. Students who are compelled to anticipate objections to their own argument and identify the flaws in those of an opponent read more carefully, think more critically, and steep themselves in relevant context, facts, and information more thoroughly. In short, using discussable text of the kind provided by every single volume in the Opposing Viewpoints series encourages close reading, facilitates reading comprehension, fosters research, strengthens critical thinking, and greatly enlivens and energizes classroom discussion and participation. The entire learning process is deepened, extended, and strengthened.

For all of these reasons, Opposing Viewpoints continues to be exactly the right resource at exactly the right time—when we most need to provide readers with the critical-thinking tools and skills that will not only serve them well in school but also in their careers and their daily lives as decision-making family members, community members, and citizens. This series encourages respectful engagement with and analysis of opposing viewpoints and fosters a resulting increase in the strength and rigor of one's own opinions and stances. As such, it helps make readers "future ready," and that readiness will pay rich dividends for the readers themselves, for the citizenry, for our society, and for the world at large.

# Introduction

> *"The thing American people fear about corporations is that they might achieve too much power. We have an antipathy to power even as we admire it."*
>
> *Annie Proulx, American novelist*

The corporatization of America is nothing new — at least fears of it happening aren't new. In an 1816 letter to his friend George Logan, Thomas Jefferson wrote of the risk of corporate power, saying that he hoped the young nation would "crush . . . the aristocracy of our monied corporations which dare to challenge our government to a trial of strength, and to bid defiance to the laws of their country." Imagine what Jefferson would have thought if he had watched Mark Zuckerberg, the founder and head of Facebook, testifying before the U.S. Congress about the company's business practices and the responsibilities of the company to its users and to the public at large. Or if Jefferson could have known that in the nation he helped to found, a handful of companies would one day dominate many major industries, including insurance, publishing, communications, and the airline and automotive industries.

Not everyone agrees that this is bad. Some feel that capitalism should be completely unrestrained. Others worry about the harm that might come to people and the planet as a result. But as wages stagnate, the divide between the rich and everyone else continues to widen, and attempts to address crucial issues such as climate change and poverty seem to stall at the door to the corporate suite, a majority of Americans have begun to think that corporations have too much power. In this volume, a variety of authors address the issue of corporate power and how it is currently playing out in the United States. Some argue that this is not a problem, though most see at least some issues that need correcting. The analysis of the problem and suggestions about what can and should be done about it, however, are widely divergent.

The first chapter is concerned with the basic question: "Do Corporations Have Too Much Power?" The authors discuss the complex interplay of issues surrounding that power, particularly how consolidation of corporate power and the typical structure of most corporations make it extremely difficult to solve long-term problems such as climate change. These authors are neither condemning nor despairing, however. You will discover many ideas for how both capitalism and the planet might be saved.

The second chapter zeroes in on democracy itself, asking, "Is Corporate Power a Danger to Democracy?" The viewpoints here focus primarily on the consolidation of the media by a few giant corporations. The fact that media is paid for by advertising from other corporations complicates things even further. Here, the authors look at other ways of funding media and analyze the weaknesses of the United States' approach while acknowledging the risks of letting the government have too much control of media. Other viewpoints in this chapter take a look at the relationship between democracy and business: Are they good for each other?

In the third chapter, the authors turn to the question of scientific and medical research and ask "Does Corporate Influence Taint Medicine and Scientific Research?" Viewpoints in this chapter address how the pharmaceutical industry can manipulate and even corrupt medical research, how much regulation is necessary and appropriate for healthcare markets, and how much the public does or does not trust scientific research when companies are involved.

The fourth chapter, "Do Tech Companies Have Too Much Power?" turns to what you might call the 500-pound gorilla ("Where does a 500-pound gorilla sleep? Wherever it wants.") in American life: the tech industry. Facebook (now Meta), Google,

Amazon, and Apple now have an outsized share of money and power over not only business and to some degree politics, but over our daily lives. The viewpoints in this chapter take a look at that situation and debate the risks and benefits of breaking up these large companies, an idea that is being discussed in Congress. In addition, one viewpoint looks at the fact that the billionaire owners of big tech often give money to charitable causes, though in terms of percentage, they typically give less than many middle-class donors.

These are all fascinating and difficult issues, and few of the viewpoints in *Opposing Viewpoints: The Corporatization of America* claim to have the final answers. But they do offer interesting and enlightening ways of thinking about issues that American citizens need to be thinking about.

OPPOSING VIEWPOINTS® SERIES

Chapter 1

# Do Corporations Have Too Much Power?

# Chapter Preface

Some of the most serious problems facing the world today—climate change, inequality, the spread of misinformation, and divisiveness—are things that large corporations are at least in part responsible for or have the power to address. Yet there is little or no control on the limits of large corporations. Big corporations are usually owned by shareholders who have invested money in the company in the hopes of getting a return on that investment. The corporation is responsible for making sure these investors make money.

This seems a straightforward way to fund a business, especially one that takes a lot of money to operate. However, this model has some unintended consequences. The primary problem is that a company's leaders must concentrate on making regular (quarterly or yearly) profits for their investors. They aren't free to make decisions that would benefit society, the world, and the environment in the long run if those actions wouldn't make money in the short run. This can lead to large corporations taking actions that are bad for everybody except their shareholders. For example, climate change is not a problem that can be solved in time for the next quarterly report to investors. Addressing it will require long-term strategies and investments, and in the short term demands sacrifice and expense—something most corporate structures aren't ready to give.

Holding companies accountable for their decisions is difficult for many reasons, but the one that concerns us in this chapter is the fact that a few large companies have an enormous amount of power, both politically and socially. The viewpoints here examine that power, the damage big corporations can do, and possible solutions to this problem. We open with a viewpoint arguing that corporations need to change their value systems, along with a few suggestions about how they might go about doing that.

> *"For today's value-minded executives, creating value cannot be limited to simply maximizing today's share price."*

# Today's Companies Need to Focus on Long-Term Values

*Marc Goedhart and Tim Koller*

*Citizens are increasingly losing confidence in large corporations. Part of the solution, the authors of this viewpoint write, is for corporations to focus on long-term value creation, rather than making as much profit as possible for their shareholders in the short term. However, the authors also argue that focusing on long-term values will benefit not just society, but corporations and their stakeholders as well. Though not every problem can be solved by shifting the focus from short-term to long-term goals, many of the issues facing society can be improved with this change. Marc Goedhart and Tim Koller work for McKinsey & Company, a global management consulting firm.*

As you read, consider the following questions:

1. What do the authors mean by "value creation"?
2. What is the difference between a stakeholder and a shareholder?

"The Value of Value Creation," by Marc Goedhart and Tim Koller, McKinsey & Company, June 16, 2020. This article was originally published by McKinsey & Company, www.mckinsey.com. 

3. What are public-benefit corporations, and why are they mentioned in this viewpoint?

Challenges such as globalization, climate change, income inequality, and the growing power of technology titans have shaken public confidence in large corporations. In an annual Gallup poll, more than one in three of those surveyed express little or no confidence in big business—seven percentage points worse than two decades ago.[1] Politicians and commentators push for more regulation and fundamental changes in corporate governance. Some have gone so far as to argue that "capitalism is destroying the earth."[2]

This is hardly the first time that the system in which value creation takes place has come under fire. At the turn of the 20th century in the United States, fears about the growing power of business combinations raised questions that led to more rigorous enforcement of antitrust laws. The Great Depression of the 1930s was another such moment, when prolonged unemployment undermined confidence in the ability of the capitalist system to mobilize resources, leading to a range of new policies in democracies around the world.

Today's critique includes a call on companies to include a broader set of stakeholders in their decision making, beyond just their shareholders. It's a view that has long been influential in continental Europe, where it is frequently embedded in corporate-governance structures. The approach is gaining traction in the United States, as well, with the emergence of public-benefit corporations, which explicitly empower directors to take into account the interests of constituencies other than shareholders.

Particularly at this time of reflection on the virtues and vices of capitalism, we believe it's critical that managers and board directors have a clear understanding of what value creation means. For today's value-minded executives, creating value cannot be limited to simply maximizing today's share price. Rather, the evidence points to a better objective: maximizing a company's value to its shareholders, now and in the future.

## Section 1: Answering Society's Call

Recently, the US Business Roundtable released its 2019 "Statement on the purpose of a corporation." Dozens of business leaders (the managing director of McKinsey among them) declared "a fundamental commitment to all of our stakeholders [emphasis in the original]." Signatories affirmed that their companies have a responsibility to customers, employees, suppliers, communities (including the physical environment), and shareholders. "We commit to deliver value to all of them," the statement concludes, "for the future success of our companies, our communities and our country."

### A Focus on the Future

The Business Roundtable's focus on the future is no accident: issues such as climate change and income inequality have raised concerns that today's global economic system is shortchanging the future. We agree. The chief culprit, however, is not long-term value creation but its antithesis: short-termism. Managers and investors alike too often fixate on short-term performance metrics, particularly earnings per share, rather than on the creation of value over the long term. By prioritizing (or, perhaps more correctly, mischaracterizing) shareholders' best interests in terms of beating analyst estimates on near-term quarterly earnings, the financial system can seem to institutionalize a model that cares only for today and all but ignores tomorrow. There also is evidence, including the median scores of companies tracked by McKinsey's Corporate Horizon Index from 1999 to 2017, that the tendency toward short-termism has been on the rise. Certainly, the roots of short-termism are deep and intertwined. A collective commitment of business leaders to clear the weeds and cultivate future value is therefore highly encouraging.

Companies that conflate short-termism with value creation often put both shareholder value and stakeholder interests at risk. Banks that confused the two in the first decade of this century precipitated a financial crisis that ultimately destroyed billions of dollars of shareholder value. Companies whose short-term focus leads to environmental disasters also destroy shareholder value, not just directly through cleanup costs and fines but via lingering reputational damage. The best managers don't skimp on safety, don't make value-destroying decisions just because their peers are doing so, and don't use accounting or financial gimmicks to boost short-term profits. Such actions undermine the interests of shareholders and all stakeholders and are the antithesis of value creation.

### Value Creation Is Inclusive

For companies anywhere in the world, creating long-term shareholder value requires satisfying other stakeholders as well. You can't create long-term value by ignoring the needs of your customers, suppliers, and employees. Investing for sustainable growth should and often does result in stronger economies, higher living standards, and more opportunities for individuals. It should not be surprising, then, that value-creating capitalism has served to catalyze progress, whether by lifting millions of people out of poverty, contributing to higher literacy rates, or fostering innovations that improve quality of life and lengthen life expectancy.

A strong environmental, social, and governance (ESG) proposition also creates shareholder value.[3] For example, Alphabet's free suite of tools for education, including Google Classroom, not only seeks to help equip teachers with resources to make their work easier and more productive, but it can also familiarize students around the world with Google applications—especially those in underserved communities who might otherwise not have access to meaningful computer engagement at all. Nor is Alphabet reticent about choosing not to do business in instances that it deems harmful to vulnerable populations; the Google Play app store now prohibits apps for personal loans with exorbitant annual percentage rates, an all-too-common feature of predatory payday loans.[4]

Similarly, Lego's mission to "play well"—to use the power of play to inspire "the builders of tomorrow, their environment and communities"—has led to a program that unites dozens of children in rural China with their working parents. Programs such as these no doubt play a role in burnishing Lego's brand throughout communities and within company walls, where, it reports, employee motivation and satisfaction levels beat 2018 targets by 50 percent. Or take Sodexo's efforts to encourage gender balance among managers. Sodexo says the program has increased the retention of not only employees, by 8 percent, but also clients, by 9 percent, and boosted operating margins by 8 percent as well.[5]

## Section 2: Shareholders and Stakeholders: A Balanced Approach

Inevitably, there will also be times when the interests of all of a company's stakeholders are not complementary. Strategic decisions of all kinds involve myriad trade-offs, and the reality is that the interests of different groups can be at odds with one another. Implicit in the Business Roundtable's 2019 statement of purpose is concern that business leaders have skewed some of their decisions too much toward the interests of shareholders.

### Stakeholders for the Long Term

Time will tell how they act on this conviction. As a starting point, we'd encourage leaders, when there are trade-offs to be made, to prioritize long-term value creation, given the advantages it holds for resource allocation and economic health. Consider employee stakeholders. A company that tries to boost profits by providing a shabby work environment, underpaying employees, or skimping on benefits will have trouble attracting and retaining high-quality employees. Lower-quality employees can mean lower-quality products, reduced demand, and damage to the brand reputation.

More injury and illness can invite regulatory scrutiny and more union pressure. Higher turnover will inevitably increase training costs. With today's mobile and educated workforce, such a company will struggle in the long term against competitors offering more attractive environments. If the company earns more than its cost of capital, it might afford to pay above-market wages and still prosper, and treating employees well can be good business.

How well is well enough? A long-term value-creation focus suggests paying wages that are sufficient to attract quality employees and keep them happy and productive and pairing those wages with a range of nonmonetary benefits and rewards. Even companies that have shifted manufacturing of products such as clothing and textiles to low-cost countries with weak labor protection have found that they need to monitor the working conditions of their suppliers or face a consumer backlash.

Or consider how high a price a company should charge for its products. A long-term approach would weigh price, volume, and customer satisfaction to determine a price that creates sustainable value. That price would have to entice consumers to buy the products—not just once, but multiple times, for different generations of products. The company might still thrive at a lower price point, but there's no way to determine whether the value of a lower price is greater for consumers than the value of a higher price to shareholders, and indeed to all corporate stakeholders, without taking a long-term view.

## Social Consequences

Far more often, the lines are gray, not black or white. Companies in mature, competitive industries, for example, grapple with whether they should keep open high-cost plants that lose money, just to keep employees working and prevent suppliers from going bankrupt. To do so in a globalizing industry would distort the allocation of resources in the economy, notwithstanding the significant short-term local costs associated with plant closures. At the same time, politicians on both sides of the aisle pressure companies to keep failing plants open. Sometimes, the government is also a major customer of the company's products or services.

In our experience, managers not only carefully weigh bottom-line impact but also agonize over decisions that have pronounced consequences on workers' lives and community well-being. But consumers benefit when goods are produced at the lowest possible cost, and the economy benefits when operations that have become a drain on public resources are closed and employees move to new jobs with more competitive companies. And while it's true that employees often can't just pick up and relocate, it's also true that value-creating companies create more jobs. When examining employment, we found that the US and European companies that created the most shareholder value in the past 15 years have shown stronger employment growth.[6]

## Section 3: Value Creation Is Not a Magic Wand

Long-term value creation historically has been a massive force for public good, just as short-termism has proved to be a scourge. But short-termism isn't the only source for today's sense of crisis. Imagine, in fact, that short-termism were magically cured. Would other foundational problems suddenly disappear as well? Of course not. There are many trade-offs that company managers struggle to make, in which neither a shareholder nor a stakeholder approach offers a clear path forward. This is especially true when it comes to issues affecting people who aren't immediately involved with the company. These so-called externalities—perhaps most prominently, a company's carbon emissions affecting parties that otherwise have no direct contact with the company—can be extremely challenging for corporate decision making because there is no objective basis for making trade-offs among parties.

That's not to say that business leaders should just dismiss the problem of externalities as unsolvable, or something to be solved on a distant day. Punting is the essence of short-termism. With respect to the climate, some of the largest energy companies in the world, including BP and Shell, are taking bold measures right now toward carbon reduction, including tying executive compensation to emissions targets.

Still, the complexity is obvious for any individual company striving to comprehensively solve global threats such as climate change that will affect so many people, now and in the future. That places bigger demands on governments and investors. Governments can create incentives, regulations, and taxes that encourage a migration away from polluting sources of energy. Ideally, such approaches would work in harmony with market-oriented approaches, allowing creative destruction to replace aging technologies and systems with cleaner and more efficient sources of power. This trading off of different economic interests and time horizons is precisely what people charge their governments to do.

Institutional investors such as pension funds, as stewards of the millions of men and women whose financial futures are often at stake, can also play a critical supporting role. In the case of climate change, longer-term investors concerned with environmental issues such as carbon emissions, water scarcity, and land degradation are connecting value and long-term sustainability. Indeed, investor scrutiny has been increasing. Long-term-oriented companies must be attuned to long-term changes that will be demanded by both investors and governments, so that they can adjust their strategies over a five-, ten-, or 20-year time horizon and reduce the risk of stranded assets, or those that are still productive but not in use because of environmental or other issues.

Unfortunately, governments and long-term investors don't always play their roles effectively. Breakdowns can lead to divergences between shareholder value creation and the impact of externalities. Failure to price or control for externalities will also lead to a misallocation of resources. Those effects can create new stresses, and sometimes outright divisions, between shareholders and other stakeholders.

Yet as the Business Roundtable statement affirms, the interests of shareholders and stakeholders can go hand in hand. Businesses make a vital contribution by creating value for the long term.

Doing so in a sustainable manner calls for meeting the concerns of communities (including the environment), consumers, employees, suppliers, and shareholders alike. A short-term focus necessarily shortchanges some or all of these constituencies. A long-term commitment toward value creation, by contrast, almost axiomatically takes a broad range of constituent interests into account. Of course, it's not the cure for all social ills (beware of anything that purports to be!), but a commitment to long-term value creation is something worth valuing indeed.

## Notes

1. An annual Gallup poll in the United States showed that the percentage of respondents with little or no confidence in big business increased from 27 percent in 1997 to 34 percent in 2019, and those with "a great deal" or "quite a lot" of confidence in big business decreased by five percentage points over that period, from 28 percent to 23 percent. Conversely, those with "a great deal" or "quite a lot" of confidence in small business increased by five percentage points over the same period (from 63 percent in 1997 to 68 percent in 2019). For more, see "Confidence in institutions," Gallup, gallup.com.
2. George Monbiot, "Capitalism is destroying the earth. We need a new human right for future generations," Guardian, March 15, 2019, guardian.com.
3. Sheila Bonini, Timothy M. Koller, and Philip H. Mirvis, "Valuing social responsibility programs," McKinsey Quarterly, July 2009, McKinsey.com; Witold Henisz, Tim Koller, and Robin Nuttall, "Five ways that ESG creates value," McKinsey Quarterly, November 2019, McKinsey.com.
4. Yuka Hayashi, "Google shuts out payday loans with app-store ban," Wall Street Journal, October 12, 2019, wsj.com.
5. Diversity & inclusion at Sodexo: Making a world of difference, Sodexo, 2018, sodexo.com.
6. We've performed the same analyses for 15- and 20-year periods and with different start and end dates and have always found similar results.

Viewpoint 2

> *"As the world warms, growing numbers of CEOs are pushing for more ambitious policy interventions to tackle the climate emergency."*

# Corporations Can Be a Force for Good in Fighting Climate Change

*Matt Gitsham, Ajit Nayak, and Jonathan Gosling*

*When people think of the role of corporate lobbying in climate change, many think of the money the oil and gas industry spent to lobby against climate policies. However, the authors of this viewpoint argue that more and more CEOs are lobbying for more government action on climate change through more ambitious policy interventions. Some of the policies corporations are lobbying for include introducing carbon taxation, increasing the use of renewable energy sources instead of fossil fuels, and banning some high-carbon activities. CEOs and corporate leaders who lobby for greater government climate intervention feel that they should use their influence to make positive change, and that a healthier and more stable society will benefit their companies. Matt Gitsham is a professor of sustainable development and human rights at Hult International Business School. Ajit Nayak is an associate professor of strategy at the University of Southampton. Jonathan Gosling is an emeritus professor of leadership studies at University of Exeter.*

"Here's How to Convince CEOs to Support Government Climate Change Action at the Expense of Their Own Profits," by Matt Gitsham, Ajit Nayak, and Jonathan Gosling, The Conversation, November 11, 2021. https://theconversation.com/heres-how-to-convince-ceos-to-support-government-climate-action-at-the-expense-of-their-own-profits-170292.

As you read, consider the following questions:

1. What are some of the corporations listed in this viewpoint that were involved in developing the United Nations (UN) sustainable development goals?
2. What data did the authors use in writing this viewpoint and making their conclusions?
3. What are some of the arguments CEOs gave for why they choose to lobby for greater government action to prevent climate change?

There is now widespread consensus that limiting the global temperature increase to 1.5°C requires fundamental changes in sectors like energy, food, transport, construction and finance towards more environmentally friendly production and consumption. This could include, for example, shifting towards a 100% renewable energy system, or replacing fossil fuel-powered vehicles with electric ones.

Government action is seen as crucial to helping support and coordinate this transition. But one key barrier has been lobbying by powerful corporate interests, who are concerned that government intervention might increase their costs and perhaps even eliminate their industries altogether. The millions spent on lobbying against climate policies by the oil and gas industry is a prime example.

But as the world warms, growing numbers of CEOs are pushing for more ambitious policy interventions to tackle the climate emergency. To investigate why the corporate lobby might be changing its stance, we looked at business involvement in the development of the UN sustainable development goals between 2012 and 2015.

Several high-profile multinational companies were involved in developing the goals, including Unilever, Nestlé, GSK, Aviva and Pearson. Many advocated strongly for which specific goals should be achieved, and what role governments should play in achieving them.

We reviewed 25 documents communicating corporations' views, and observed nine meetings between business leaders and policymakers. We also conducted 57 interviews with 45 CEOs and senior executives representing 30 companies involved in this process.

We found that many companies were making strong calls for ambitious government intervention towards fighting climate change, through a mix of public investment, financial incentives and regulation.

For example, many were calling for governments to introduce carbon taxation (taxing greenhouse gas emissions to help low carbon alternatives become cheaper) and to move towards banning certain high-carbon activities (such as putting a date on when petrol cars or gas boilers can no longer be sold). Many companies

## Corporations Green Up

To move toward cleaner energy without sending power plants into premature retirement, companies are making over plants, switching fuels, and boosting efficiency. Some utilities are "repowering" coal plants . . . to run on cleaner natural gas or biomass; nearly 50 units are slated for retrofits in the U.S. alone. "Repowering" is an industry term, but the concept also applies to trucks, buildings, and land. For businesses loath to see valuable assets become obsolete, it's a no-brainer. California garbage hauler Ratto Group is replacing the guts of 17 diesel trucks with electric systems that will meet state air regulations. "This gives me the ability to keep the vehicles that I currently have," says COO Lou Ratto, "and keep these things going for as long as I want to."

Many answers on climate change might lie in a cloud—the virtual one. As part of President Barack Obama's Climate Data Initiative, tech giants such as Google, Microsoft, and Amazon are lending their computational muscle to crunch data on the environment and help communities plan for an altering landscape. The results—from drought maps to sea-level charts—can help also pushed for government subsidies for fossil fuels to be ended and given to renewable energy projects instead.

## Corporate Goals

Conventional wisdom tells us that corporate lobbying tends to be focused on weakening government intervention. However, the leaders we spoke to justified their lobbying for increased government intervention by arguing that the world sorely needed sustainability transitions across multiple industries.

Many leaders felt they had a responsibility to use their influence to encourage these transitions. This included calling for more ambitious intervention from governments, even if that added costs in the short term.

Others argued that businesses require a thriving, stable society to operate, and cannot survive in a failing world. And in some

farmers manage crops or officials steer construction projects away from flood zones.

A warming world isn't likely to change money—but it could affect how people invest it. Banks are now offering "green bonds," which let investors link their money to environmental causes. Green bonds are similar to regular bonds, but they fund projects that mitigate climate change or help people adapt to it. "We're telling the investor exactly how the money will be used," says World Bank sustainability adviser Laura Tlaiye.

Clean-energy proposals qualify, as do innovations in waste management and agricultural efficiency. In Rio de Janeiro $600 million went to improve a traffic-alleviating suburban rail network. Belarus borrowed $90 million to replace natural gas heating with biomass. U.S. banks have created their own green bonds; earlier this year one leading bank raised half a billion dollars to finance cities' plans for new solar capacity, wind turbines, and energy-efficient street lamps.

**"Businesses," National Geographic.**

cases, increased public investment, incentives and regulation could grow markets, encouraging companies to align environmental responsibility with commercial incentives.

For example, renewable energy subsidies helped grow the market for solar panels on roofs; regulations banning the sale of petrol cars increase the market for electric cars; and taxing carbon could help grow the market for low-carbon alternatives like LED lighting.

## Life Experiences

So why don't all companies devote time and energy to lobbying for more government action? When pressed on this point, many CEOs took the conversation in a different direction, citing personal life experiences as a cause of their lobbying.

These included being personally exposed to climate-related suffering, having been the target of NGO campaigning, and being challenged to engage by others: from other CEOs and non-executive directors, senior political figures and public intellectuals to their own children.

Often these experiences were linked to participation in climate networks, such as the UN Global Compact—a non-binding pledge encouraging businesses to commit to sustainability. We call this action in response to being challenged by others "the echo of conscience."

As the public continues to hold corporate leaders to higher and higher standards, our work suggests how we can encourage more CEOs to push governments towards radical climate action. People involved in working towards sustainability transitions must enlist CEOs to positively influence one another's decisions through sustainability-focused CEO networks.

We must create opportunities for CEOs to have first-hand experiences of the problems caused by their industry's impact on climate—as well as opportunities for CEOs to be personally challenged by respected figures and people they care about, especially their children. Finally, we need to encourage corporate HR departments to focus on these elements in leadership selection and development, to make sure those who lead the world's companies are also leading the world towards a brighter future.

Viewpoint 3

> *"Businesses operate on short-term objectives of profit maximisation and shareholder return."*

# Emphasis on Short-Term Profits Is Incompatible with Addressing Climate Change

*Christopher Wright and Daniel Nyberg*

*In this viewpoint, the authors warn that leaving the problem of addressing climate change to businesses is unlikely to do much good. The authors' research found that even when businesses make bold pro-climate proposals, they soon revert to their same old harmful ways. In general, the authors found that corporate climate leadership tends to follow the same pattern: a corporation frames tackling climate change as a business opportunity, then they try to establish more localized and concrete plans, and then eventually companies return to business as usual without significant changes to their policies. Christopher Wright is professor of organizational studies at the University of Sydney and Daniel Nyberg is professor of management at the Newcastle Business School of the University of Newcastle.*

"Why We Can't Rely on Corporations to Save Us from Climate Change," by Christopher Wright and Daniel Nyberg, The Conversation, October 27, 2017. https://theconversation.com/why-we-cant-rely-on-corporations-to-save-us-from-climate-change-86309. 

As you read, consider the following questions:

1. What about the way business managers operate makes tackling climate change difficult, if not impossible, according to this viewpoint?
2. How do corporations attempt to make a "business case" for climate friendly actions?
3. What examples do the authors give of pressure from stockholders and others causing companies to abandon climate action and revert to business as usual?

While businesses have been principal agents in increasing greenhouse gas emissions, they are also seen by many as crucial to tackling climate change.

However, our research shows how corporations' ambitious pro-climate proposals are systematically degraded by criticism from shareholders, media, governments, other corporations and managers.

This "market critique" reveals the underlying tension between the demands of tackling climate change, and the more basic business imperatives of profit and shareholder value. Managers operate within increasingly short time frames and demanding performance metrics, due to quarterly and semi-annual reporting, and the shrinking tenure of executives.

Our research involved detailed analysis of five major Australian corporations over ten years, from 2005 to 2015. During this period, climate change became a central issue in political and economic debate, giving rise to a range of risks and opportunities for business.

Each of the companies we studied acted at the leading edge of this issue. However, despite operating in different industries (banking, media, insurance, manufacturing and energy) we found a common pattern in which initial statements of climate leadership degenerated over time into more mundane business concerns.

Our study revealed three phases to this transformation.

## 1. Climate Change As a Business Opportunity

In this first phase, senior executives present tackling climate change as a strategic business decision.

This is epitomised by British entrepreneur Richard Branson, who has claimed that "our only hope to stop climate change is for industry to make money from it."

The managers in our study associated climate change with words like "innovation", "opportunity", "leadership" and "win-win outcomes." At the same time they ruled out more negative or threatening associations, such as "regulation" or "sacrifice."

For example, in outlining why his company had embraced the climate issue, the global sustainability manager of one of the world's largest industrial conglomerates told us:

> We're eliminating the false choice between great economics and the environment. We're looking for products that will have a positive and powerful impact on the environment and on the economy.

## 2. Localising Climate Engagement

These statements of intent are open to criticism from customers, employees, the media and competitors, especially with respect to the substance and relevance of corporate climate action.

Thus, in the second phase, managers sought to make their proposals more concrete through eco-efficiency practices (such as reducing energy consumption, retrofitting lighting, and using renewable energy), "green" products and services, and promoting the need for climate action.

Notably, these are often supplemented with measures of corporate worth to demonstrate a "business case" for climate action (for instance, savings from reduced energy consumption, increased employee satisfaction and engagement, or improved sales figures from green products and services).

Importantly, companies also sought to communicate the benefits of these measures to employees through corporate culture change initiatives, as well as to customers, clients, NGOs and political parties.

As the environment manager at the global media company we studied outlined, these practices were central to creating a climate-conscious culture in his organization:

> That inspires others and it gets things done. It's a fantastic tool. It's how behavioural change happens on sites.

## 3. Normalisation and Business As Usual

Over time, however, climate initiatives attracted renewed criticism from other business groups, shareholders, the media, and politicians.

For instance, the increasingly heated political debate over carbon pricing forced many companies to rethink their public stance on climate change.

As a senior manager at one of the country's major banks explained:

> How we deal with sensitivities within the organisation about taking what can be seen as a partisan position in a highly political environment . . . that's the challenge at the moment.

And so, in the third phase we found that climate change initiatives were wound back and market concerns prioritised.

At this stage, the temporary compromise between market and social/environmental discourses was broken and corporate executives sought to realign climate initiatives with the goal of maximising shareholder value.

For example, new chief executives were promoted who advocated "back to basics" strategies. Meanwhile, climate change initiatives were diluted and relegated to broader and less specific "sustainability" and "resilience" programs.

One of our case study companies is a large insurance company. While initially very progressive on the need for climate change action, this changed after a reversal in its financial situation and a change of leadership.

As a senior manager explained:

> Look, that was all a nice thing to have in good times but now we're in hard times. We get back to core stuff.

## Where Next from Here?

These case studies, on top of our previous research, show why corporations are particularly unsuited to tackling a challenge like climate change.

Businesses operate on short-term objectives of profit maximisation and shareholder return. But avoiding dangerous climate change requires the radical decarbonisation of energy, transportation and manufacturing on a scale that is historically unprecedented and probably incompatible with economic growth.

This means going beyond the comfortable assumptions of corporate self-regulation and "market solutions," and instead accepting regulatory restrictions on carbon emissions and fossil fuel extraction.

It also requires a reconsideration of corporate purpose and the dominance of short-term shareholder value as the pre-eminent criteria in assessing business performance. Alternative models of corporate governance, such as B corporations, offer pathways that better acknowledge environmental and social concerns.

In an era in which neoliberalism still dominates political imaginations around the world, our research shows the folly of depending on corporations and markets to address climate change.

Viewpoint 4

> *"Analysts should focus their white-boarding exercises on developing business models that correlate every dollar made with a measurable unit of social or environmental improvement."*

# To Truly Do Good, Businesses Need to Overhaul Their Business Models and Corporate Cultures

*Nishant Bagadia*

*We have seen viewpoints arguing that corporations are responsible for much of the climate change problem and that the corporate model is ill-suited to addressing it. The previous viewpoint mentioned B corporations (or benefit corporations) as an alternative corporate structure. Here, Nishant Bagadia takes a closer look at B Corps and finds that while they are valuable, more is required to create deep social good. He also offers suggestions for how to do that. Some of the suggestions he makes include tying revenue to social or environmental benefits and shifting the focus from shareholder return. Nishant Bagadia is a researcher and consultant focused on exploring the intersection of tech and social impact.*

"Can Corporations Inspire Social Good?" by Nishant Bagadia, Stanford Social Innovation Review, March 16, 2018. Reprinted by permission.

As you read, consider the following questions:

1. What are B Corps, and how are they different from traditional corporations?
2. What is "shareholder supremacy" and how did it get enshrined in U.S. law?
3. What is "trickle-up economics" as described here, and what is that being contrasted with?

Can corporations produce social good while operating within the bounds of market-based capitalism? Recent headlines would indicate yes—at least on the face of it.

Corporate giants Amazon, Berkshire Hathaway, and J.P. Morgan announced a new, independent health care company in late January that will remain "free from profit-making incentives and constraints"—a move that leverages their corporate reach to ensure long-term economic and social equality by offering low cost medical care for millions of people. Separately, BlackRock CEO Larry Fink recently sent his annual letter to thousands of BlackRock's portfolio CEOs, saying that "to prosper over time, every company must not only deliver financial performance, but also show how it makes a positive contribution to society." As the world's largest investment management firm with $6.3 trillion in assets under management, BlackRock certainly draws attention when it suggests how a company can deliver better financial performance. But why would an investment firm or Fortune 100 company care about producing social good?

Corporations can improve societies and the environment without neglecting their bottom line, according to the model developed by Jay Coen Gilbert's nonprofit, B Lab. Gilbert's team created the B Impact Assessment, a scorecard that measures a company's social good on a 200-point scale. To date, B Lab has certified nearly 2,500 B Corporations, or B Corps, and has advocated for a new corporate entity called the benefit corporation, now legally recognized in 33 US states. B Corps are obliged to create measurable positive impact in addition to maintaining financial return. In an article for Forbes, Gilbert opines that if Amazon and its newfound partners form their health care entity as a certified B Corp, they can "build trust with a skeptical public through radical transparency, ensure that the [new health care] company remains purpose-driven over the long term, and demonstrate that we can use the power of the markets to solve our most challenging problems."

While I agree that a B Corp is a valuable template for moving beyond shareholder priorities, I argue that creating true social good requires deeper business and cultural transformations to help organizations effectively navigate market constraints.

## From Shareholder to Multi-Stakeholder Capitalism

In 1919, Ford Motor Company founder Henry Ford advocated for repurposing his company's revenue into investments that would benefit employees and fund business production, rather than provide returns for shareholders. However, Ford's largest shareholders, John Francis Dodge and Horace Elgin Dodge, sued him for neglecting to make dividend payments.

The ensuing *Dodge v. Ford Motor Co.* court case marks a historical moment, as the judge ruled that "a business corporation is organized and carried on primarily for the profit of the stockholders." Ever since, the concept of "shareholder supremacy" has dominated US capitalism, driving a culture of public investments in corporate stocks and fashioning what some have called a "shareholder nation." Untouched and unregulated, this model of ownership breeds inequality, as seen today when the richest 1 percent of Americans now own a staggering 45 percent of the country's wealth. As Gilbert says, unless a legal mandate shifts corporate responsibility to "benefit for all stakeholders, not just shareholders," capitalism will continue to emphasize profit over public good.

## Deeper Business and Cultural Transformations

I believe "multi-stakeholder" capitalism requires even further organizational renovation. A legal delegation and B Certification may serve as critical starting points for companies like Amazon and BlackRock to catalyze change. But becoming a B Corp on paper is not enough. Companies must craft a socially impactful culture to shape the everyday practices of the employees, managers, and consumers involved in fulfilling an organization's purpose. The following business strategies can help:

### 1. Develop a business model that binds revenue to social or environmental benefits.

As seen with the Gap's child-labor scandal or Unilever's handling of mercury exposure in its Indian factories, it is detrimental to companies if they maintain business models that reap billions of dollars from damaging production methods or non-sustainable goods. No wonder that one of the popular critiques of corporate social responsibility (CSR), which I define as a company's programmatic effort to create sustainable business practices, is that these programs often operate in silos or serve as a proxy to offset profit-maximizing operational strategies. Instead, analysts should focus their white-boarding exercises on developing business models that correlate every dollar made with a measurable unit of social or environmental improvement.

One relevant example is Guayaki Brands. Guayaki produces organic Yerba Mate teas and energy drinks harvested natively from rainforests in Central and South America. Systematically, Guayaki claims that every one pound of yerba mate purchased decreases atmospheric carbon dioxide by 573 grams. Its "market driven restoration business model" also provides farming communities with a renewable income stream based on regenerative, soil-enriching, and carbon-reducing planting techniques.

As a consumer, Guayaki's business model helps me associate my positive environmental impact to every ounce of yerba mate I purchase. It also provides what co-founder David Karr calls "trickle up economics, whereby a company invests in healthy people, healthy land, and healthy communities" that ensure long-term environmental and economic sustainability.

**2. Inspire socially good consciousness.**

Is a brand recognized for its positive social or environmental impact? Is a company invoking what I call a "socially good conscience"? Meaning, a brand not only is recognized for doing good, but also motivates others to act and think in a socially or environmentally responsible manner. If not, the future of that business could be in danger.

Because in this evermore connected society, we are all looking for companies that can help guide us toward long-term global sustainability. Millennials—the generation that makes up the largest percentage of the US (and global) workforce and drives trillions of dollars in consumer spending—actively invest in, work for, and purchase from companies that prioritize social purpose along with financial growth.

Most of all, millennials want a brand to be inspirational.

Take, for example, the outdoor clothing company Patagonia, a brand that inspires activism with its vocal and timely environmental conservation campaigns. This includes viral Internet campaigns such as the recent "The President Stole Your Land" response to Donald Trump's elimination of nearly two million acres of protected land. This week, Patagonia took its advocacy one step further: It launched the Patagonia Action Works platform. This tool provides people with an easy way to find local events, volunteer opportunities, causes, and petitions for relevant conservation and community issues. Patagonia also implements best-in-class workforce and gender-equality standards, which have become a model for other companies and have created a highly sought-after culture that attracts millennials to both its products and its workforce.

## Correcting Capitalism

Amazon and BlackRock are planting a seed. But correcting capitalism requires that companies go beyond shareholder return, beyond multi-stakeholder engagement, and beyond changing legal structure. It requires that companies create a business model and culture that drives our conscious desire to do good. Consumers will embrace companies that set forth actionable policies, products, and tools. To quote former President Barack Obama: "The single most important thing I could do would be to help prepare the next generation of leaders to take their own crack at changing the world." Indeed, if an organization can inspire us to do good, we will in turn inspire others to do the same.

## Periodical and Internet Sources Bibliography

*The following articles have been selected to supplement the diverse views presented in this chapter.*

Ayana Archie, "The Founder of Patagonia Is Giving His Company Away to Help Fight Climate Change," NPR, September 15, 2022. https://www.npr.org/2022/09/15/1123104499/patagonia-founder-climate-change.

Milan Babic, Eelke Heemskerk, and Jan Fichtner, "Who Is More Powerful: States or Corporations?" the *Conversation*, July 10, 2018. https://theconversation.com/who-is-more-powerful-states-or-corporations-99616.

Mallen Baker, "A Worthy Niche Project That Won't Change the World," *Innovation Forum*, June 11, 2021. https://www.innovationforum.co.uk/articles/b-corps-a-worthy-niche-project-that-won-t-change-the-world.

Milton Friedman, "A Friedman Doctrine: The Social Responsibility of Business Is to Increase Its Profits," *New York Times*, September 13, 1970. https://www.nytimes.com/1970/09/13/archives/a-friedman-doctrine-the-social-responsibility-of-business-is-to.html.

Lisa Herzog, "Corporate Knowledge and Corporate Power: Reigning In the Power of Corporations as Epistemic Agents," *Critical Review of International Social and Political Philosophy*, August 21, 2022. https://www.tandfonline.com/doi/full/10.1080/13698230.2022.2113227.

David Leonhardt, "The Jack Welch Effect: His Ruthlessness as General Electric's CEO Was Ultimately Bad for the Company, A New Book Argues," *New York Times*, June 5, 2022. https://www.nytimes.com/2022/06/05/briefing/jack-welch-david-gelles.html.

George Monbiot, "Capitalism is Killing the Planet: It's Time to Stop Buying into Our Own Destruction," *Guardian*, October 30, 2021. https://www.theguardian.com/environment/2021/oct/30/capitalism-is-killing-the-planet-its-time-to-stop-buying-into-our-own-destruction.

Michael O'Leary and Warren Valdmanis, "How the 137 Million Americans Who Own Stock Can Force Climate Action," *Vox*, October 15, 2020. https://www.vox.com/21509913/climate-change-bp-microsoft-investors-shareholders-accountability.

Ciara Torres-Spelliscy, "The Power Corporations Have in Changing Laws," NPR, April 2, 2021. https://www.npr.org/2021/04/02/983925056/the-power-corporations-have-in-changing-laws.

Kevin A. Young, Tarun Banerjee, and Michael Schwartz, "The Secret to Corporate Power," *Yes!*, July 13, 2020. https://www.yesmagazine.org/democracy/2020/07/13/corporate-power-politics.

OPPOSING VIEWPOINTS® SERIES

Chapter 2

# Is Corporate Power a Danger to Democracy?

## Chapter Preface

A free press is essential to a free society. Democracy can't survive without it. However, media outlets have been increasingly consolidated and bought up by large corporations or tech billionaires. Jeff Bezos, founder and owner of Amazon, one of the nation's four largest tech giants, owns the *Washington Post*, one of the nation's premier newspapers. Though Bezos has so far kept to his promise of staying clear of the editorial side of the paper's business, his ownership of the paper is still troubling to many.

However, the biggest issue with corporate control of media is less the ownership of the outlets themselves than the business model. News organizations depend on advertising revenue from companies to stay in operation. Those companies have some control, if not direct control, over what the news outlets publish.

The viewpoints in this chapter provide an in-depth discussion of the one form of media in the United States that does not depend on advertising for its revenue: the Corporation for Public Broadcasting, the agency behind Public Broadcasting Station (PBS) and National Public Radio (NPR). Though these media organizations are free from the need to court and please advertisers, they get very little government funding. This means that they must frequently resort to canvassing viewers and listeners for support. In theory this sounds good, as the public they are meant to serve pays for the service. However, much of the public that would benefit from the service cannot afford to donate to the stations. As one author in this chapter points out, that means the stations are forced to cater to people who can afford to donate rather than the general public.

Not all the conversation here is about media. In this chapter, you'll also read viewpoints that argue that free-market capitalism is good for democracy and that democracy is good for markets, along with viewpoints exploring the public's views on corporate power and democracy.

Viewpoint 1

> *"To be economically viable, therefore, public media must focus on affluent, educated listeners. The result is a media system that can, at times, seem woefully out of the touch with the nation it purports to represent."*

# For Public Media to Serve the Public, It Must Get More Government Funding

*Christopher Chávez*

*In this viewpoint, Christopher Chávez points out that though public media in the U.S. was founded as a way to get news and information to "the uneducated, the poor, the housebound, ethnic minorities and those living in rural areas," its content now is tailored primarily for high-income baby boomers. Chávez argues that the reason for this is due to the fact that because the Corporation for Public Broadcasting (CPB) gets so little funding, it is dependent on donations from listeners, and not all listeners can afford to contribute. Christopher Chávez is an associate professor of communications at the University of Oregon.*

As you read, consider the following questions:

1. What were the original mandates of the Corporation of Public Broadcasting?

"Why America's Public Media Can't Do Its Job," by Christopher Chávez, The Conversation, May 3, 2017. https://theconversation.com/why-americas-public-media-cant-do-its-job-75044. 

2. How is British public media supported?
3. According to Chávez, how would boosting funding for public media make it more likely to fulfill its mission of serving the public at large?

When the Trump administration released its proposed budget in March, it suggested eliminating federal funding for the Corporation of Public Broadcasting (CPB).

"Can we really continue to ask a coal miner in West Virginia or a single mom in Detroit to pay for these programs?" Trump's Office of Management and Budget director, Mick Mulvaney, said in defense of the cuts.

Mulvaney seemed to argue that public media was a luxury for the educated few, rather than a truly public resource. Indeed, since the CPB was first established, the degree to which public media reflects the diversity of the nation has the subject of much debate.

But it's not as simple as Mulvaney makes it out to be. Though the proposed cuts seem unlikely to go through this year, public media will continue to be at the mercy of political and economic factors that have hampered its ability to fulfill its mission and achieve its goals.

## A Mirror for the Nation

When Congress passed the Public Broadcasting Act of 1967 to establish a national, publicly funded media system, there were two clear mandates: to cultivate a more engaged citizen and to affirm the nation's diversity.

In the network's original mission statement, NPR architect Bill Siemering described public media as a "necessity for citizens in a democratic society to be enlightened participants." Unbeholden to the demands of the marketplace, public media would ideally be able to reach audiences that might not be targeted by commercial broadcast networks and their advertisers. This included communities traditionally left out of civic discourse: the uneducated, the poor, the housebound, ethnic minorities and those living in rural areas.

"We try to mirror ALL of the country—perhaps the hardest thing of all," NPR's former deputy director Rick Lewis said in 1970, describing his vision for "Morning Edition."

To tackle this challenge, the CPB decided its subsidiaries, National Public Radio (NPR) and the Public Broadcasting Service (PBS), would have a national reach. Meanwhile, they would cultivate member stations rooted in a diverse range of communities across the country. NPR affiliates based in Fresno, California; Mobile, Alabama; or Erie, Pennsylvania might all carry national programs, but they are also tasked with pursuing local stories.

## A Precarious Funding Model

Nonetheless, speaking to the country's extraordinarily diverse populations through a single media system has proven tricky. And over the years, public media has ended up tailoring its programs to an almost exclusively upscale audience of baby boomers.

The decision to focus on college-educated listeners and viewers is certainly a function of the CPB's own economic realities. As communications professor Robert McChensney argued in his book *The Political Economy of Media* American public media has been severely handicapped since its inception.

Unlike the British Broadcasting Corporation (BBC)—which citizens subsidize by paying an annual television license fee—American public media receives relatively little federal funding, denying it a stable source of income. With federal funding in a constant state of flux, public media has come to rely on income from private sources such as pledge drives and corporate underwriting accounts. For example, in 2015 NPR member stations received about 14 percent of their revenues from federal, state and local entities, while 20 percent came from corporations and 37 percent from private donations.

To be economically viable, therefore, public media must focus on affluent, educated listeners. The result is a media system that can, at times, seem woefully out of the touch with nation it purports to represent.

Just as the country is becoming more ethnically, religiously and linguistically diverse (a recent Pew study showed that the U.S. electorate in 2016 was the most diverse in the nation's history), consumers of national public media remain disproportionately white.

According to a 2012 report, the audience for NPR's member station news programs was 5 percent African-American, 6 percent Latino and 5 percent Asian-American. This disparity is also reflected at the leadership level. In an essay, Joseph Tovares, the senior vice president and chief content officer for the CPB, admitted that the inclusion of African-Americans, Latinos, Asian Americans and Native Americans at the general manager level are almost nonexistent at NPR and PBS member stations.

We see these disparities in the programming itself. Like other national media institutions, public media has traditionally struggled to find a way to include the voices of ethnic and racial minorities. While there are some bright spots—including PBS's children's programming and NPR's Latino USA, the overall diversity efforts seem tepid. In a forum organized by NPR to address public radio's diversity challenges, sociologist Michael Schudson effectively captured the dilemma:

> No doubt the staff makes an effort to cover issues of special importance to minorities and women, but you suspect that it is a mission and not a habit, and that it feels like a kind of foreign correspondence. You know it can be done well or poorly but, in either case, it is done with the handicap of a largely monochromatic newsroom.

## A Wavering Commitment to Diversity?

Public media realizes that the status quo is a losing strategy. The demographic realities are too sobering. NPR projects that by 2020, its stations' audience of people younger than 45 will be around 30 percent—half of what that audience accounted for in 1985.

To its credit, the CPB has made broadening its appeal a core part of its current strategy, which includes what it calls the "three D's": digital, diversity and dialogue.

However, their own strategic documents provide some insight into just how elastic their definition of inclusion is. For example, NPR's target audiences still include the "Affluent Business Leader" who is "a c-level employee, has an investment portfolio of $150,000 or more, and holds a leadership position in a club or organization." Then there's the "Cultural Connoisseur" who has a postgraduate degree, is more likely to buy tickets for classical music, ballet and opera, and takes more than three vacations a year. For its part, PBS touts the "Power Mom," who enjoys outdoor activities and spends a significant amount of time online searching for information on museums and concerts.

In other words, these are not the disenfranchised communities whom the original architects of NPR believed would be served by public media.

As journalism professor Ralph Engelman writes in his book *Public Radio and Television in America* today's public media was born out of the desire to achieve a more democratic version of German philosopher Jürgen Habermas' public sphere. Habermas' notion of what "public" means was criticized as being reserved for propertied, educated males at the exclusion of the poor and disenfranchised. But by serving those already inclined to participate in civic life, it appears that today's public media extends—rather than disrupts—this pattern.

Just as we're witnessing unprecedented attacks on the country's most disenfranchised communities, this seems like an institutional failure. Legislators are advancing policies designed to restrict the movements of Latinos and Muslims. Gains made by the LGBTQ community are being scaled back. There are active efforts to dismantle the Affordable Care Act, eliminate entitlement programs and defund early education programs like Head Start, all of which undermine working-class communities.

Now more than ever, it seems necessary to include the voices—and reach the people—most impacted by these policies. It seems that only by unhitching its funding model from private interests can public media truly fulfill its mission of serving the public at large. But this would require a federal government that's willing to boost—rather than slash—its funds.

Viewpoint 2

> *"The political capture of mass media happens by governments, political parties and big corporations and creates a worsening situation for those who are at the margins of the society."*

# Corporate and Government Control of Media Stifles Democracy and Crushes Dissent

*Data Leads*

*This viewpoint from Data Leads begins with a statement about the role of the media in informing public opinion—and for supporting democracy and giving a voice to dissent. However, how well the media does this is often determined by who owns or controls the media, and media can be used to stifle dissent and restrict democracy as well as to give it a voice. The discussion here is limited to the political situation in India, but the basic argument applies to countries around the world, including the United States. Data Leads is a digital media and information initiative aimed to help people understand and engage with the world around them. It is based in India.*

As you read, consider the following questions:

1. According to this viewpoint, what are the results when media is owned by people with political or party links?

"A Delicate Handshake," Data Leads, Media Ownership Monitor, May 16, 2022. https://india.mom-rsf.org/en/findings/politicalaffiliations/. 

2. Other than direct ownership, what does this viewpoint mention as a way for government to control media?
3. Is there a difference between the effects of government control of media and corporate control? Why or why not?

Media is one of the potent tools to launch a robust political narrative in any society. The information that is relayed and then consumed by the audience has a direct bearing on the public opinion. This information is critical for a democracy to survive and dissent to thrive. However, in India, there has been a worrying trend in recent times, when media has, more often than not, come under scrutiny for drifting away from its purpose to relay information and refrain from catering to any specific interests.

The association of power with media goes back a long way. Control of media has been instrumental in manufacturing public consent and controlling dissent. This control of the information space can happen through a variety of channels. Direct control by imposing strict laws and legislation that limit the scope of what can be reported, influence through state funding such as for advertisement or covertly by the way of owning the media. The latter is a subtle and innocuous way of controlling the political discourse and limiting critical reportage. Additionally urging media outlets to perform self-censorship through several pressure strategies happens to be a tool for control.

## Media Owners with Political Links

The Indian media landscape has changed significantly over the last decade. With the advances in technology, the media industry has been burgeoning like never before and expanded its reach, in terms of the number of outlets, whether in television, radio or newspaper. While this has set an impressive trend for market growth, the underlying consequences of this rapidly growing media landscape has thrown up a few challenges as well. The people with access to the corridors of power have been successful in influencing dissemination of information through media houses, by partially owning these outlets, and tangentially influencing the way the news is presented. Clearly, ownership of the media significantly affects the perspectives presented in the reporting and bias becomes inevitable in such circumstances.

Within the sample of this study, as many as ten media owners have direct or indirect links with politics while some of them even represent a political party. There are countless others however, who have refused to declare their political affiliations, but yet own media companies. Between them, media owners with political links control a sizeable share of viewership/readership.

Since August 2016, Dr. Subhash Chandra, Zee News' co-owner, is an independent Member of Rajya Sabha, the Upper House of the Indian Parliament, though he got elected with the help of Bharatiya Janata Party, BJP lawmakers in the state of Haryana. Zee Media Corporation Limited (ZMCL) owns Zee News, which is among the top four Hindi news channels in the country and largely perceived to be sympathetic to the BJP, and its brand of politics.

Rajeev Chandrashekar is a member of BJP, the ruling Bhartiya Janata party and represents it as a member of the Rajya Sabha. He pioneered Republic TV, which commands a sizable percentage of the English news segment. Although he formally resigned from the board of the broadcaster, citing his involvement in the political party as a reason for his disengagement, the channel has never been able to shake off its perception of being a BJP-friendly television news outlet. Chandrasekhar's Jupiter Capital Private Limited also directly owns two south Indian news channels—Asianet News in Malayalam and Suvarna News in Kannada.

Various regional news channels are also partly or wholly owned by politicians. One of the reasons that politics and media are closely intertwined in these regions could be the fact that regional political parties are playing an important role in India as they are particularly strong in reaching the masses, and national parties like the Congress and the BJP, partner with regional players during elections. These strong political outfits eventually chose to have their own mouthpieces, the media outlets. There are quite a few examples: Baijayant 'Jay' Panda, is a former member of the Biju Janata Dal, BJD, a regional party in Odisha and has been in power for five terms. Today 'Jay' Panda is the BJP national vice president and official spokesperson of the party and in addition is a co-owner of Odisha TV. Mahendra Mohan Gupta, owner of *Dainik Jagaran* —a Hindi newspaper, is a member of Parliament, Rajya Sabha. Supriya Sule, director of *Sakal*—a Marathi newspaper, is an Indian politician from the Nationalist Congress Party and member of the Indian Parliament in the Lok Sabha. Another politician, Himanta Biswa Sarma, a Minister in the BJP Government in the state of Assam, is the husband of Riniki Bhuyan Sarma, who owns and operates the news television channel News Live.

It is starkly evident that media is owned by those people who have direct access or are in close proximity to power. Their media channels are likely to rather focus on influencing and creating opinions than on the unbiased dissemination of information. The ownership by people with political connections could easily impact news dissemination, leading to a perception of being potential propaganda machines that serve the agenda of a certain political ideology or thought.

## Dependence of Media on Government Advertising

Apart from the direct ownership, advertising can present another form of potential control over editorial content since more and more media show greater dependence on advertisement revenues. Therefore, it is probably fair to say that Indian media, these days, is rather profit than conviction driven.

This dependency becomes highly problematic, when media houses earn additional money through carrying, in particular, government advertisements. This contributes to the spread of their agenda. Through the media houses' financial dependency on state advertisements, they toe the line of producing a favourable coverage for the government.

A transparent and independent coverage of content gets compromised a great deal by ways of such "soft pressure." Often, there is an invisible pressure, for a newspaper, or a television channel to articulate the point of view of the government in a contentious issue.

According to 2017 figures, the Department of Audio-Visual Publicity, the government department that allocates government advertisements to print outlets, spends as much as INR 21.34 million / USD 0.32 million for Hindi and INR 14.09 million/ USD 0.202 million for English print advertising. Government advertising therefore is the bread and butter for many but in particular for smaller Hindi newspapers allowing the government to exploit its advertisement spending and the subsequent financial dependency of media outlets as a means of control. The financial struggles of several media companies to sustain with their business model makes them more vulnerable to such dependencies and therefore control mechanisms.

Potentially, if it so desires, the government of the day can give advertising to those whom they would like to reward. And conversely, those newspapers, which have earned their ire, can easily be punished by the government by cutting down on the advertising being given to them. Room for influencing the public advertising allocations results from the process through which it is determined and which lacks accountability. It relies upon circulation data approved by the DAVP (Directorate of Audio Visual Publicity). These figures depend on a certified Chartered Accountant's testimony, which establishes the "official" number of copies printed. However, there is no scope for a physical check of the number of newspapers printed in India as the numbers of newspapers and TV channels have massively increased throughout the years. As per the latest figures, there are 380 plus TV news stations and 118,239 publications, which include 17,239 dailies.

Also in TV, as the distribution of government advertising is based on ratings, there is room for doubt because these ratings are established without any transparency or accountability by an industry-owned association. Moreover, the audience shares of the top four TV channels are extremely close to each other and critics allege that the allocation of government advertising on TV is arbitrary.

On top of "official" state advertising comes the one of political parties and it is no surprise that BJP, the ruling party, is the biggest advertiser in the past five years. According to the Broadcast Audience Research Council (BARC) the party had 22,099 insertions (number of times an ad is aired on TV) in less than one week (between November 12 to 16, 2018), which was almost twice as much as the second largest advertiser in the country—Netflix. BJP ads ranked number one across all channels in the five states that went into assembly elections at the end of 2018—Madhya Pradesh, Rajasthan, Chhattisgarh, Telangana and Mizoram. The BJP ranked number two for the preceding week, while the Congress party did not even feature in the top-ten list.

As an obvious result, media owners, quite aware of the political leverage through advertising, toe the official government's and BJP's line both in TV and print. There is clearly less coverage of the opposition.

## Need to Regulate Political Capture of the Media

The increasing control of the media by the government and the ruling party is an ubiquitous phenomenon that has come in handy to have a hold on the public. Apart from stifling the discourse and limiting the freedom of opinion, it has also blinded the people from knowing their real interests. The political capture of mass media happens by governments, political parties and big corporations and creates a worsening situation for those who are at the margins of the society. It leads one to the most significant question of whether there should be a legislation banning big corporations and politician to own media. As the space for critical commentary is shrinking at a fast pace there is an urgent need to address the issue.

Because it is mainly invisible to the publics' eye, media ownership is one of the least appreciated factors contributing to the threat of the press freedom and compromising of ethical journalism. According to the Free Press Unlimited, the ownership of media by people who have vested interests has enabled the governments and corporations "to develop a centralized information strategy that amounts to a modern form of propaganda whereby all important media are speaking a similar vocabulary, demonizing the same enemies, and presenting the same arguments in support of the leadership's actions."

Today, there are no regulatory safeguards against political control over media in India. The Indian laws do not restrict political ownership in television or print media with the exception of radio, where political parties or members thereof are disqualified from applying for a license to operate a radio station. However, radio is barred from broadcasting independent news. There is no mandatory requirement to disclose political affiliations of the owners or of their family members.

Viewpoint 3

> *"Strong growth in certain repressive systems, especially China, has given the misleading impression that authoritarianism is good for business."*

# Democracy Is Good for Business

*Sarah Repucci*

*We have heard from authors discussing the effect of business on democracy. In this viewpoint, Sarah Renucci discusses the effect of democracy on business and argues that democracy is good for business. Despite the impression given by countries such as China, she argues that repressive governments are not good for business. A more democratic world offers greater stability and more opportunities for corporations to thrive. At the time she wrote this viewpoint, Sarah Repucci was vice president of research and analysis at Freedom House, an organization devoted to the support of democracy around the world.*

As you read, consider the following questions:

1. Why has China's strong economic growth been misleading about the importance of democracy to business?
2. According to this viewpoint, why is long-term political stability essential for business growth?

"Democracy Is Good for Business," by Sarah Repucci, Freedom House, August 3, 2015. Reprinted by permission.

3. According to this viewpoint, in what ways do authoritarian governments inhibit economic growth?

Recent diplomatic breakthroughs involving Iran and Cuba could pave the way for major investment by U.S. companies. But despite the excitement generated when an isolated and repressive regime begins to open up its market, an open political system would be much better for business.

Stable, transparent governments built on respect for human rights and the rule of law tend to foster environments that are conducive to the establishment and unfettered operation of private enterprises. This is clearly illustrated in the World Bank's *Doing Business* survey and Freedom House's *Freedom in the World* report: On average, countries that perform well in one assessment also excel in the other.

Conversely, regimes that oppress their populations are more likely to limit business opportunities. According to *Doing Business*, governments in countries identified as Not Free in *Freedom in the World* generally impose more red tape, build up barriers to trade, and fail to enforce contracts.

The correlation suggests that established democracies could serve their own economic interests by encouraging democratic institutions abroad and thereby improving the business environment over the long term.

## Image and Reality

Strong growth in certain repressive systems, especially China, has given the misleading impression that authoritarianism is good for business. The casual observer might see ruthlessly implemented development projects and probusiness legal window dressing as more important to the operating environment than things like parliamentary oversight and freedom of assembly.

However, only a handful of Not Free countries score highly on the *Doing Business* "distance to frontier" measurement, which compares economies as they are with regulatory best practice. Most Not Free states breed corruption due to their opacity and concentration of power, are prone to sudden and arbitrary decisions due to the lack of checks and balances, and are more susceptible to political unrest than democracies because they do not allow peaceful changes of government through elections. None of these traits are helpful to businesses.

A number of developing countries that are often praised for macroeconomic expansion, such as Angola, Ethiopia, and Uganda, actually receive rather low scores on *Doing Business*, and are rated Not Free by Freedom House for their repression of political opposition and other democratic shortcomings. China earns only a middling score from the World Bank report. While its sheer size and momentum have allowed it to attract massive investment on its own difficult terms, last month's stock-market plunge may have a sobering effect. Myanmar, which has been hailed as a hot investment opportunity since U.S. and European sanctions were lifted, ranks near the bottom of Doing Business and continues to imprison journalists and allow persecution of ethnic minorities. Multinational corporations are similarly eager to enter Iran once it is relieved of international sanctions under the recent nuclear agreement, but it too scores poorly on both its regulatory environment and its political rights and civil liberties.

At the positive end of the spectrum, the major democracies of South America, Europe (including newer democracies in the east), East Asia, and South Africa all promote regulatory systems that are as open as their political systems. Even Greece, despite its current struggle with excessive public debt, continues to be rated Free by Freedom House and ranks in the top third of the World Bank's report.

## Exceptions and Outliers

There are a number of governments that buck the trend, either combining political freedom and a poor business climate or managing to encourage business while simultaneously clamping

## Corporate Speech

On January 21, 2010, the Supreme Court issued what is certain to become a landmark ruling in the case of Citizens United v. Federal Election Commission. In a 5–4 ruling, the Court struck down federal limits on what organizations (including non-profit organizations, unions, and for-profit corporations) may say during elections. A ban on direct contributions to candidates was left in place. The majority reasoned that the speech limits violated the First Amendment and chilled political expression. With this ruling, the Court seemed to reverse the trend of the last century, which brought greater limits to corporate political speech and activity.

**"Citizens United v. Federal Election Commission (2010)," Bill of Rights Institute.**

down on political rights and civil liberties. Most in the latter camp are small states with the will, incentives, and sufficiently tight control to maintain these clashing priorities. Such governments also tend to treat foreigners and natives differently, welcoming multinational companies and expatriate professionals out of necessity, even as they dominate many aspects of their own citizens' lives. (Low-skilled foreign workers, of course, receive the worst treatment of all.)

Examples include Singapore as well as the Persian Gulf monarchies of Bahrain, Qatar, and the United Arab Emirates. Rwanda also scores high on *Doing Business* under President Paul Kagame's strong-arm rule; Kagame has made impressive strides against corruption and pushed through other business-friendly measures, but has chosen not to allow parallel improvements in civic and political affairs.

There are also significant democracies that have failed to foster bureaucratic efficiency and predictable conditions in which businesses can thrive. Freedom House has ranked India as Free for nearly 20 years, but the World Bank places it near the bottom on indicators such as the time required to start a business, taxes, and enforcement of contracts. Some African countries that stand out for upholding political rights and civil liberties, such as Benin and Senegal, likewise rate poorly for their business environments.

Democracy is clearly not the only factor behind good economic performance, but more often than not, it provides the long-term political stability and corrective mechanisms that form a foundation for safe investment and steady growth.

## Policy Implications

Policymakers often argue that "soft" values such as human rights and democracy must take a backseat to economic and security interests. In a recent report, *Supporting Democracy Abroad*, Freedom House found that even top-performing Sweden failed to consistently promote democracy and human rights in its trade policy.

Such prioritization is shortsighted. A more democratic world would be a more stable, inviting place for established democracies to trade and invest. The political crackdowns and security crises associated with authoritarian rule often drive out business and place employees, supply chains, and investments at risk, in addition to raising reputational and legal concerns for foreign companies that stay involved.

Therefore, democratic governments seeking to bolster the global economy and develop new markets should press their counterparts not just for lower barriers to trade and less red tape, but also for strong and accountable democratic institutions.

Viewpoint 4

> *"Americans are deeply pessimistic about the fairness of the U.S. economic system. Still, a majority of the public maintains the belief that most people can get ahead through hard work."*

# Corporations Have Too Much Power, Americans Say

*Pew Research Center*

*This viewpoint is a write-up of a survey by Pew Research Center on what Americans think of the economic system in the U.S. The findings outlined here show that majorities on both sides of the political divide believe that big corporations have too much power and make too much money. The survey also found that a large majority believe the American economic system is unfair. Yet, despite these criticisms, most Americans still believe that individuals can get ahead with enough hard work. Pew Research Center is a non-partisan organization that does public polling and demographic research.*

As you read, consider the following questions:

1. According to these findings, how does income affect people's view of corporate power?

"Views of the Economic System and Social Safety Net," Pew Research Center, December 17, 2019.

2. Which groups are most likely to say that the government should do more to help people in need?
3. This research finds that most Americans feel the economic system is unfair, yet many also think you can get ahead if you work hard enough. Does this seem like a contradiction? Why or why not?

The American public is broadly critical of the power held by major corporations in the United States and the profits made by business corporations.

Nearly three-quarters of U.S. adults (73%) say major corporations in the country have too much power; far fewer (22%) say they have the right amount of power and just 4% say they have too little power.

There is some bipartisan agreement in views of corporate power. A majority of Republicans and Republican-leaning independents (62%) say major corporations in the U.S. have too much power; an even larger majority of Democrats and Democratic leaners (83%) also hold this view.

Liberal Democrats (90%) are somewhat more likely than conservative and moderate Democrats (78%) to say corporations have too much power. Among Republicans, conservatives (59%) are 9 percentage points less likely than moderates and liberals (68%) to view corporations as too powerful.

The public also is critical of the profits made by business corporations: 65% say corporations make too much profit, compared with 33% who say they make a fair and reasonable amount of profit.

Democrats and Democratic leaners overwhelmingly say that most business corporations make too much profit (80%). By contrast, Republicans and Republican leaners are divided in their views: 48% say corporations make too much profit, while about as many (50%) say they make a fair and reasonable amount of profit.

Within the GOP there are significant divides in these views by ideology. Most conservative Republicans (59%) say business corporations make a fair and reasonable amount of profit. Views tilt in the opposite direction among moderate and liberal Republicans: 61% say business corporations make too much profit.

There are more modest differences by ideology among Democrats: 87% of liberals and 75% of conservatives and moderates say most business corporations make too much profit.

## Views of Corporate Power By Level of Household Income

Among the general public, views of corporate power are similar across income levels. For instance, 73% of those with family incomes of $100,000 a year or more and 72% of those earning less than $30,000 a year say major corporations have too much power.

However, there are income differences on this question between Republicans and Democrats, and the respective partisan patterns run in different directions.

Among Republicans and Republican leaners, lower earners are more likely to see corporations as too powerful than higher earners. For instance, 71% of Republicans earning less than $30,000 a year say corporations have too much power, compared with 52% of those earning at least $100,000 a year.

By contrast, Democrats and Democratic leaners with the lowest levels of household income are somewhat less critical of corporate power than those with higher incomes: 73% of Democrats earning less than $30,000 a year say corporations have too much power, compared with roughly nine-in-ten Democrats with incomes of $100,000 or more (91%).

As a result, higher-income Republicans and Democrats are far apart in their views on corporate power, while among lower-income Americans there is little difference between the views of Republicans and Democrats.

## Leaders in Business and Technology Get Low Marks on Empathy

In addition to concerns over corporate power and profits, the public is critical of how well leaders in business and technology understand the needs of everyday people.

Overall, 68% say business and technology leaders understand the needs of people like them either not too well (46%) or not at all well (22%). Just 31% say these leaders understand their needs very (4%) or somewhat well (27%).

Criticism of business and technology leaders on this measure is bipartisan: 71% of Democrats and Democratic leaners and 66% of Republicans and Republican leaners say leaders in technology and business do not understand the challenges they face in their own lives.

## Partisan, Demographic Differences in Views of Government Aid to Needy

Americans are divided in their views on government aid to poor and needy people, and partisan differences on these questions are among the largest seen in the survey. In addition, level of household income is tied to attitudes on these questions, with those earning less more supportive of government aid.

Overall, 40% say the government should provide more assistance to people in need, while 26% say the government should provide less assistance; 33% say the current level of assistance to people in need is about right.

A majority of Democrats and Democratic leaners (59%) say the government should provide more assistance to people in need. Three-in-ten say the current level of assistance is about right, and just 10% say the government should provide less assistance to people in need. Liberal Democrats (72%) are much more supportive of expanding aid to needy people than are conservative and moderate Democrats (49%)

Republicans and Republican leaners are far less supportive of expanded aid to people in need: 46% say the government should provide less assistance, while 37% say the current level of assistance is about right. Relatively few (17%) say the government should provide more assistance to people in need. Among conservative Republicans, 54% say the government should provide less assistance to people in need; about a third of moderate and liberal Republicans (32%) say the same.

In addition to partisan differences, views on this question diverge by age and level of household income.

Younger adults are more supportive of expanding assistance to people in need than are older adults. For instance, 46% of those ages 18 to 29 support greater government assistance, compared with 35% of those 65 and older.

Those with the lowest levels of household income are most supportive of expanding aid to people in need. A majority of those earning less than $30,000 a year (55%) say the government should provide more assistance to people in need. Support is much lower among those with annual household incomes of $30,000-$74,999 (38%), $75,000-$99,999 (28%) and $100,000 or more (34%).

Among Republicans and Republicans leaners, 37% of those earning less than $30,000 a year support greater government assistance to people in need. Among higher-earning Republicans, support for this policy is much more limited.

Among Democrats and Democratic leaners, there is a modest gap in support for more assistance to people in need between the lowest earners (64%) and the highest earners (58%). Half of those with family incomes of $75,000-$99,999 a year support this policy, as do 59% of those making $30,000-$74,999.

The public is divided on two other questions about the government's role providing aid to poor and needy people, with Republicans and Democrats holding contrasting views.

When asked which statement comes closer to their views, 50% of Americans say that "poor people have hard lives because government benefits don't go far enough to help them live decently," while roughly the same share (47%) say "poor people today have it easy because they can get government benefits without doing anything in return." About three-quarters of Republicans and Republican leaners (74%) say poor people have it easy because of the government benefits they can receive. A similar share of Democrats and Democratic leaners (72%) say poor people have hard lives because government benefits to do not go far enough.

On a related measure, 49% say the government should do more to help needy Americans, even if it means going deeper into debt, compared with 48% who say the government can't afford to do much more to help the needy. Here again, partisan differences are stark: 72% of Republicans say the government can't afford to do much more to help the needy; 67% of Democrats say the government should do more to help the needy, even if it means going deeper into debt.

## Views on Opportunity and Fairness of Economic System

Americans are deeply pessimistic about the fairness of the U.S. economic system. Still, a majority of the public maintains the belief that most people can get ahead through hard work.

Overall, 60% say that most people who want to get ahead can make it if they're willing to work hard, while 39% say that hard work and determination are no guarantee of success for most people.

The youngest adults are less likely than older adults to say people can get ahead if they're willing to work hard: 53% of those ages 18 to 29 say this. By comparison, majorities of those ages 30 to 49 (58%), 50 to 64 (61%) and 65 and older (68%) take this view.

Nearly eight-in-ten Republicans and Republican leaners (78%) believe that most people can make it if they're willing to work hard. Democrats and Democratic leaners are divided: 45% say hard work is enough for most people to get ahead, but 54% say that hard work and determination are no guarantee of success.

By about two-to-one (66% to 34%), liberal Democrats say hard work is no guarantee of success for most people. Among conservative and moderate Democrats, 56% say most people can get ahead through hard work, while 43% say hard work is no guarantee of success.

When it comes to views of the U.S. economic system, 70% say the system unfairly favors powerful interests, while just 29% say the economic system in the country today is generally fair to most Americans. A large majority of Democrats (86%) believes the economic system unfairly favors powerful interests. Republicans are evenly split: 50% say it is generally fair to most Americans, and 50% say it unfairly favors powerful interests.

Among Republicans, there are substantial differences on this question by ideology. Most conservative Republicans (58%) say the economic system is generally fair to most Americans. By contrast, 62% of moderate and liberal Republicans say it unfairly favors powerful interests.

Among Republicans, a majority of those with household incomes of less than $30,000 a year (59%) say the economic system unfairly favors powerful interests. This view is less widely held among higher earners. For instance, fewer than half of Republicans earning $100,000 a year or more (37%) believe the economic system is unfair. Lower-earning Republicans also are more likely than higher earners to say that hard work and determination are no guarantee of success for most people; however, this view remains a minority opinion among Republicans across income levels.

Among Democrats, income differences on these questions are smaller than among Republicans. But to the extent that they do exist, Democrats with lower incomes are somewhat less critical of the economic system and more positive about the ability to succeed through hard work than higher-earning Democrats.

As a result of different dynamics among Republicans and Democrats, overall income differences in views of economic fairness and the relationship between hard work and success are relatively modest. And the partisan gaps on these two questions are much larger among higher-earning Republicans and Democrats than they are among lower-earning partisans.

## Long-Term Opinion Trends: Views of the Social Safety Net and Nation's Economic System

In recent years, Pew Research Center has transitioned from probability-based telephone surveys to the American Trends Panel, a probability-based online panel. The transition from phone surveys conducted with an interviewer to online self-administered surveys brings with it the possibility of mode differences—differences arising from the method of interviewing.

This section includes opinion measures on views of the social safety net and the U.S. economic system. Several questions on these subjects have long-standing telephone trends and were included on a survey conducted in September on the American Trends Panel (ATP), on which this report is largely based, and a contemporaneous telephone survey. This allows for a comparison of any "mode effects" and places the current panel estimates in the context of telephone data.

On the American Trends Panel, 50% say poor people have hard lives because government benefits do not go far enough to help them live decently, while 47% say poor people today have it easy because they can get government benefits without doing anything in return. On the telephone survey, 52% say poor people have hard lives, compared with 36% who say they have it easy. As is often the case, the share offering no opinion is much higher on the phone survey (12%) than the online survey (3%).

The partisan gap on this question is very large, in both the phone and panel data. On the ATP, three times as many Democrats and Democratic-leaning independents as Republicans and Republican leaners say the poor have hard lives because government benefits are insufficient to allow them to live decently (72% vs. 24%). The gap between Republicans and Democrats has widened over the past two decades, largely because Democrats increasingly say the poor have hard lives because government benefits do not go far enough.

There also is a striking partisan divide in views of whether or not the government should do more to help the needy, even if it means going deeper into debt. On the American Trends Panel, 49% of the public overall says the government should do more to help the needy, even if this adds to the nation's debt; 48% say the government can't afford to do much more to help the needy. On the contemporaneous phone survey, 52% say the government should do more to aid the needy even if it raises the debt, while 40% say the government can't afford this.

In the online survey, two-thirds of Democrats and Democratic leaners say the country should to more to help the needy, even if it means increasing the debt; just 27% of Republicans and Republican leaners say the same. Partisan differences on this question today are much larger than they were throughout much of the 1990s and 2000s.

In surveys conducted online and by telephone, majorities say the nation's economic system unfairly favors powerful interests. However, on the American Trends Panel, 70% say the economic system unfairly favors powerful interests, while 29% say it is generally fair to most Americans. On the phone survey, 60% say the system unfairly favors the powerful, while 37% say it is generally fair.

There have long been sizable partisan differences on this question. Republicans are more likely than Democrats to say the economic system is fair. Half of Republicans say this on the online survey (60% on the phone survey); an overwhelming share of Democrats (86% on the ATP, 80% on the phone survey) say the system unfairly favors powerful interests.

On the American Trends Panel, nearly twice as many say that business corporations make too much profit (65%) as say most corporations make a fair and reasonable profit (33%). On the phone survey, 56% say corporations make too much profit, while 38% say profits for most corporations are fair and reasonable.

Online, nearly half of Republicans (48%) say corporations make too much profit; 36% express this view on the phone survey. Majorities of Democrats on the ATP survey (80%) and by phone (73%) say business corporations make too much profit.

For more than two decades, majorities of Americans have said that most people can get ahead if they are willing to work hard; fewer have expressed the view that hard work is no guarantee of success for most.

On the current online survey, 60% say most people can succeed through hard work, while 39% say hard work is no guarantee of success. On the telephone survey, 65% say hard work leads to success; 32% say hard work does not necessarily ensure success.

Consistent majorities of Republicans (78% on the ATP) say that hard work leads to success for most people. Democrats have long been less likely to express this view: 45% say this in the online survey.

VIEWPOINT 5

> *"Correlations and cluster analyses show that high levels of secure funding for public media systems and strong structural protections for the political and economic independence of those systems are consistently and positively correlated with healthy democracies."*

# More Funding for Public Media Would Help, but Not Enough to Heal America's Political Divide

*Joshua Benton*

*The first viewpoint in this chapter discussed the problems with the funding model for America's public broadcasting system. This viewpoint, a book review by Joshua Benton, discusses the United Kingdom's very different approach to publicly supported news and information. The term "the Beeb" is an affectionate nickname for the British Broadcasting Company (BBC), Britain's public media system. PBS and NPR are the U.S. public media for television and radio, respectively. Government support of PBS and NPR in the U.S. is fairly limited, but Benson argues that this is not just a cause of the problems with American democracy, but a symptom of it. Joshua Benton is a senior writer for the Nieman Journalism Lab.*

"Do Countries with Better-Funded Public Media Also Have Healthier Democracies? Of Course They Do," by Joshua Benton, NeimanLab, January 24, 2022. Reprinted by permission. Published by arrangement with the Neiman Foundation for Journalism.

As you read, consider the following questions:

1. How much does the U.S. spend per person each year on public broadcasting?
2. According to this viewpoint, how is market-driven media different from publicly funded media? What are the pros and cons of each?
3. This viewpoint points to research showing a correlation between a lack of support for public media and flawed democracies. What do you think accounts for this connection?

There's a new book coming out in the U.K. this week called *The BBC: A People's History*, by David Hendy. Its publisher calls it a "monumental work of popular history, making the case that the Beeb is as much of a national treasure as the NHS . . . a now global institution that defines Britain and created modern broadcasting."

Cross the pond: While Americans generally like PBS and NPR, I wouldn't expect them to come up quickly if you asked someone on the street to begin listing national treasures. (I'm even more sure America's health care system would go unmentioned, too.) Who "created modern broadcasting" in the U.S.? It certainly wasn't the two public broadcasters that didn't hit airwaves until 1970. And what TV network is a "global institution" that "defines" the United States abroad? Apologies to PBS Newshour, but that's CNN.

No one says "Auntie Peebs."

It's obvious that the U.S. approached the new broadcasting technologies of the 20th century in ways wildly different from their European peers—and in ways that reflect on the countries themselves. American radio began wild and unregulated, experimental, a bubbling font of creativity—and then quickly became commercialized, optimized for mass audiences and massive profits. The BBC, which turns 100 this year, was more structured, more statist, more controlled—but has remained more central to residents' lives, more civic-minded, and more beloved.

Those different visions of public service broadcasting have affected how we get our news. But do they also affect something deeper—civic life, or democracy itself?

That's the subject of a new paper out in The International Journal of Press/Politics. It's titled "Funding Democracy: Public Media and Democratic Health in 33 Countries" and it's by Timothy Neff and Victor Pickard, both of Penn. (Well, they were both of Penn; Neff just moved to the University of Leicester, crossing that pond the other way.)

The abstract:

> This study examines whether and how public media systems contribute to the health of democracies in 33 countries in Europe, Africa, Asia, North America, the Middle East, Latin America, and South America.
>
> We gather national economic data and public media funding levels, audience shares, and regulatory data, primarily for 2018 and 2019 but in some cases earlier, due to lack of available data. We then assess correlations with strength of democracy indices and extend Hallin and Mancini's typology of North American and European media systems through hierarchical cluster analysis of these 33 countries.
>
> We find five models of public media systems around the world, ranging from "state-administered" systems with low levels of independence (Botswana and Tunisia) to systems aligning with Hallin and Mancini's "Democratic Corporatist" model, with strong and secure (multiyear) funding, large audience shares, and strong regulatory protection for their independence. In between, we identify three mixed models: a "Liberal-Pluralist" model, a "Direct Funding" model, and a "Commercial–Public" model.
>
> Correlations and cluster analyses show that high levels of secure funding for public media systems and strong structural protections for the political and economic independence of

> those systems are consistently and positively correlated with healthy democracies.

So maybe not the best sign for American democracy then.

The Hallin and Mancini referenced are Daniel C. Hallin (he of the spheres) and Paolo Mancini, authors of the media-studies classic *Comparing Media Systems: Three Models of Media and Politics*. They argued that the interactions between politics and media are affected not just by individual players or institutions (a Murdoch or a *New York Times*) but by the structures of a country's broader media system—something influenced by government regulation, political history, technology, geography, and the market, among other things.

Neff and Pickard are interested in the public broadcasting piece of those systems. The most obvious way to measure the importance a country puts on a public broadcaster is how much money, per capita, it spends on it. And among rich countries, the United States is a biiiiiiiig outlier. It's like the rest of the world is playing high-level soccer and we're off in a corner, doodling with a ketchup bottle.

Germany spends $142.42 per person on its public media. Norway spends $110.73, Finland $101.29, Denmark $93.16. Leave Scandinavia for Western Europe and you see the U.K. at $81.30, France at $75.89, and Spain at $58.25. Heading a bit east? The Czech Republic's at $60.08, Estonia $55.70, and Lithuania $32.71.

Only trust the Anglosphere? Try Australia $35.78, New Zealand $26.86, or Canada $26.51. How about Asia? Japan spends $53.15, South Korea $14.93. Africa? Botswana's at $18.38, Cabo Verde $15.22.

And then there's the United States—which spends $3.16, per person, per year, on public broadcasting. Ten quarters, four dimes, five nickels, and a penny.

> The U.S. is a clear outlier in having the world's largest GDP while its public media receives a well-below-average of $9.87 in per capita funding and $3.16 in per capita public funding.

> Higher ratios [of public media support to GDP] show larger disparities between public media funding per capita and GDP per capita. Only Taiwan's GDP–funding ratio (7,089; Table 1) exceeds the U.S. ratio (6,380).
>
> Figure 1 also shows that countries in Latin America and South America have exceptionally large ratios. Two of these countries—Chile and Colombia—have primarily commercial-funded public media systems. Most ratios in other countries in our study remain within a narrow range (Cabo Verde's 306 and Israel's 1,670).

So that's measuring inputs—funding. What about outputs? What share of their media consumption time do people in their countries spend consuming public media?

> Audience share data also show great disparities among the world's public media, with shares again tending to be higher in Western European countries (e.g., 40 percent in Norway and 35 percent in Sweden) but also in sub-Saharan Africa (e.g., 35.6 percent in Botswana, 38 percent in Cabo Verde, and 38 percent in South Africa).
>
> Countries in Latin America and the Caribbean have public media with far lower market shares (e.g., 0.4 percent in Uruguay and 2 percent in Argentina). North American public media also are outliers (5.1 percent share in Canada and 2 percent share in the U.S.).

"But Josh," you might be saying, "the United States is different." And that's true! With a large population, the world's lingua franca, and lots of money, there's no shortage of private media companies eager to serve up whatever the market demands. If your goal is to give people access to high-quality media, you can indeed count on the private sector more in the U.S. (330 million people, $62,997 GDP/capita) than in Botswana (2.3 million people, $18,064 GDP/capita), or even countries like Norway, which are plenty rich but still small and relatively language-isolated.

But the tradeoff, of course, is that market-driven news organizations act differently than public-supported ones. There are positive elements to both, but the BBC is unlikely to start pushing ivermectin because it thinks there's a market opportunity on the far right.

Neff and Pickard take a variety of external ratings of the health of each country's democratic institutions and mash them up with all this data—plus more information about the funding structures, editorial independence, and other factors at play—to see how connected public media and civic health are.

> This analysis shows five clusters of public media systems, which we have descriptively labeled.
>
> These range from "State-administered" systems with low levels of independence (Botswana and Tunisia) to systems aligning with Hallin and Mancini's "Democratic Corporatist" model, with generally strong and secure (multiyear) funding, large audience shares, and strong regulatory protection for their independence (Norway, Sweden, U.K., Iceland, and Germany, with Mauritius and Denmark as outliers with less public funding as a proportion of revenues and weaker regulatory protection).
>
> In between, we identify three mixed models…
>
> …a "Liberal-Pluralist" model, which mixes countries in Hallin and Mancini's "Liberal" and "Polarized Pluralist" models and includes public media systems that have, on average, moderate levels of less secure funding, weaker regulatory protections, and small audience shares (New Zealand, Canada, Uruguay, Argentina, Spain, and France)…
>
> …a widespread "Direct Funding" model encompassing most of the other public media systems in this study with funding directly linked to their publics in the form of license fees or equivalent taxes (though this funding is at a moderate level and is less secure than funding in the Democratic Corporatist model) and which is accompanied by generally strong regulatory protections and high audience shares (Ireland, Italy, Cabo Verde, South Korea, and South Africa in a subgroup with less public funding as a proportion of all funding; Israel, Czech Republic,

> Japan, Finland, and Lithuania in a subgroup with more public funding as a proportion of all funding)...
>
> ...a "Commercial–Public" model, often found among EIU's1 "flawed" democracies, in which public media systems are, on average, more reliant on commercial funding and have small audience shares (U.S., Australia, Estonia, Taiwan, Latvia, and India, with strongly commercial Chile and Colombia outliers in this cluster).

Always good to make a list of "flawed" democracies. Who wants perfection, anyway?

Neff and Pickard find significant correlations between public media funding levels and democratic health. (Of note, they didn't find significant correlations between public broadcasters' audience share and democratic health. In other words, the benefits of a robust public broadcaster come from the simple fact that it exists—a centering anchor in the media marketplace—not only that it attracts a big audience.)

> ...our research shows that countries near the top of EIU's Democracy Index have well-funded public media with substantial footprints in their national media systems, and these public media tend to meet minimal criteria for regulatory and funding frameworks that assure autonomy and stable financial support.
>
> Even as revenues for commercial media organizations dropped precipitously over the past two decades, countries with robust public media systems maintained strong positions in EIU's rankings.
>
> However, the U.S. dropped from "full democracy" to "flawed democracy" in 2016 (EIU 2020b) and has continued to decline (score of 8.22 in 2006 and 7.96 in 2019).
>
> Such patterns, if broadly understood, may compel American citizens—and especially policymakers—to reexamine commonly held assumptions about the relationships between media subsidies and democracy.

Many people—Pickard in particular—have called for public funding to fill the voids created by the decline of commercial news, especially local commercial news, in the United States. As he put it in his Nieman Lab prediction for this year: "In 2022, we will confront a stark choice: Either we build non-market systemic support for local journalism, or we condemn entire communities to a future of news deserts."

As you might imagine, I agree that more public money for local journalism is a great idea. But I don't think the direction of causality is at all clear here. Is America a "flawed" democracy because we don't fund public media? Or does America not fund public media because we're a flawed democracy?

It would, after all, be pretty on brand for the United States to build a system that relies on corporations seeking profits to meet public needs; to rely on our size and wealth to create and extend cultural hegemony; to put knowledge important to public debate behind a paywall; to view national unity as something to feed with rhetoric but not dollars.

There is a long line of research into the relationship between a state's heterogeneity—how diverse its population is in terms of ethnicity, religion, language, and so on—and the relative size of the social safety net it is willing to fund. In essence, the more a country's people see themselves as part of a unified us, the more likely they are to fund more generous social programs. The more they see their country through a Tucker Carlson lens—as a nightmarish mix of blood-sucking immigrants, ethnic others, and people who don't look or act or sound like you—the less likely they are to want to chip in.

It's no accident that the American states with the worst racial histories are also the ones that offer the weakest social safety nets. It's not surprising that Scandinavian countries—long places of relative unity in terms of race, religion, and language—fund larger welfare states as well as more robust public media. And it's also not surprising that, as those countries have grown more diverse, their safety nets are starting to tear.

Public broadcasters are part of a nation's media-political system—but they're also a result of it. More public funding of media would do some wonderful things on the ground to create more informed and engaged communities. But I suspect that even multiplying public funding 10× would do little to bridge the deeper divides in the American public that led to their underfunding in the first place.

Viewpoint 6

> *"There is a growing body of research that suggests substantial social benefits from strong public media systems, including well-informed political cultures, high levels of support for democratic processes, and increased levels of civic engagement."*

# Repairing Media Could Help Repair Democracy

***Alina Ladyzhensky***

*The author of the previous viewpoint did not think that publicly funded media could do enough to salvage the U.S. political system for its destructive divisiveness. This viewpoint by Alina Ladyzhensky is an interview with Victor Pickard and Timothy Neff, two professors whose work focuses on public media in America. They think that public media can help restore American democracy, and their research suggests there are many social benefits to strong public media. At the time this viewpoint was published, Alina Ladyzhensky, who conducted the interview, was associate director of communications for the Annenberg School of Communications at the University of Pennsylvania.*

"Public Media Can Improve Our 'Flawed' Democracy," by Alina Ladyzhensky, Annenberg School for Communication (University of Pennsylvania), March 16, 2022. Reprinted by permission.

As you read, consider the following questions:

1. According to research cited by Pickard and Neff, what are the advantages of a strong public media?
2. Why does corporate funding not provide the advantages of strong public media? What are the motivations of corporate-funded media and why are they not aligned with the public good?
3. What are arguments against public funding of public media?

Thousands of newspapers across the U.S. have shuttered or downsized in recent years, leaving many communities without—or with highly diminished—local news outlets. The collapse of local journalism and rise of 'news deserts,' along with the spread of dis- and mis-information, all point to a news industry in crisis.

As commercial news continues experiencing structural and financial issues, media scholar Victor Pickard, Ph.D., the C. Edwin Baker Professor of Media Policy and Political Economy and Co-Director of the Media, Inequality & Change (MIC) Center at the Annenberg School for Communication, advocates for a promising alternative: increased government investment in nonprofit and public media.

Scholarship by Pickard and others finds that public media has myriad social benefits, including more diverse news coverage, increased public knowledge about politics and public affairs, and lower levels of extremist views. Building on this, a new study co-authored by Pickard and Timothy Neff, Ph.D., reveals that countries with independent and well-funded public broadcasting systems also consistently have stronger democracies.

The study, "Funding Democracy: Public Media and Democratic Health in 33 Countries," shows that while other democracies have recognized the value of public media systems, America is a major outlier. Despite having the world's largest gross domestic product

(GDP), America spends a comparatively miniscule fraction— less than half of a percent—on public media funding.

As newsrooms around the country continue to dwindle, a well-informed and politically engaged public is essential for democracy to thrive. In this Q&A, Pickard and Neff, a former MIC postdoctoral fellow and now a lecturer in Journalism at the University of Leicester, explain how democratic health is determined, how the U.S. ranks against other countries, and how our media infrastructure can be changed for the better.

**How did you choose which countries to analyze for this study?**

**TN:** We selected 33 countries that spanned *The Economist*'s Democracy Index's seven global regions. Our selection criteria favors countries ranked as either full or flawed democracies, rather than authoritarian regimes, as well as countries that enable comparisons across different types of national media systems. We correlated these countries' democratic rankings with their levels of public media funding and with regulatory structures that support their financial and political independence.

**What are the factors you looked at to determine the health of a democracy?**

**TN:** We relied on *The Economist*'s Democracy Index, which measures health across five key dimensions of democracies: electoral process (freeness and fairness of elections); functioning of government (determination of policy by freely elected leaders, without undue influence by other powers or corruption); political participation (citizen engagement with democratic processes); political culture (public support for democracy); and civil liberties (media freedom, freedom to associate, and support for human rights).

**Where is the U.S. positioned in terms of democratic health and public media funding, as compared to other countries?**

**VP:** According to *The Economist's* Democracy Index, the U.S. is now considered to be a "flawed democracy." In terms of its public media funding, it is almost literally off the chart for how little it allocates towards its public media compared to other democracies around the planet. It comes out to .002 percent of Gross Domestic Product (GDP). At $465 million dollars, 2020 federal funding of U.S. public media amounted to just $1.40 per capita. Meanwhile, countries such as the UK, Norway, and Sweden spend close to $100 or more per capita toward their public media.

**According to your research, how can public media help strengthen democracies?**

**VP:** While our research specifically shows the correlation between strong public media systems and strong democracies, there is a growing body of research that suggests substantial social benefits from strong public media systems, including well-informed political cultures, high levels of support for democratic processes, and increased levels of civic engagement.

**What are some arguments against government support of public media? How do you counter these criticisms?**

**VP:** There is a common fear, especially here in the U.S., that government funding of public media creates a dangerous situation where our news organizations will become mouthpieces of the state. While state capture is a legitimate concern, many democracies around the world have figured out how to create strong safeguards to maintain public media's independence. Moreover, our research bolsters the argument that a robust public media system is beneficial—perhaps even essential—for maintaining a healthy democratic society.

**What are your recommendations for the future of public media funding and infrastructure in the U.S.?**

**VP:** Since the market is no longer supporting the level of news media—especially local journalism—that democracy requires, there is arguably now an even stronger case to make that public media needs to step into the vacuum to address the widening news gaps as the commercial newspaper industry continues to wither away. News deserts are expanding across the country and around the world. This should be public media's moment—an opportunity to revisit its core purpose and assess how it should operate within a democratic society and within an increasingly digital media system. Ideally, we would both restructure and democratize our public media system as we expand this critical infrastructure.

## Periodical and Internet Sources Bibliography

*The following articles have been selected to supplement the diverse views presented in this chapter.*

Daniella Ballou-Aares, David Clunie, and Rhett Buttle, "American Democracy Is Under Threat. Business Leaders Must Act to Ensure Safe and Fair Elections," Black Economic Alliance, June 6, 2022. https://blackeconomicalliance.org/news/american-democracy-is-under-threat-business-leaders-must-act-to-ensure-safe-and-fair-elections/.

Rolf Brühl and Benedikt Kapteina, "Fighting for Democracy: The Case for Corporate Political Responsibility," London School of Economics and Political Science, May 6, 2022. https://blogs.lse.ac.uk/businessreview/2022/05/06/fighting-for-democracy-the-case-for-corporate-political-responsibility/.

Jerry Davis, "Why Big Tech's Swift Reaction to the Capitol Riot Is a Threat to Democracy," *Fast Company*, January 20, 2021. https://www.fastcompany.com/90596158/big-tech-capitol-rioters-corporate-power.

Sandra Knispel, "Corporate Money in Politics Threatens US Democracy—or Does it?" University of Rochester News Center, July 6, 2020. https://www.rochester.edu/newscenter/does-money-in-politics-threaten-us-democracy-442802/.

Joel Kotkin, "The Fascist Threat Was Never Trump—It's Corporate Power," *Daily Beast*, December 2, 2020. https://www.thedailybeast.com/the-real-fascist-threat-was-never-trumpits-corporate-power.

David Leonhardt, "A Crisis Is Coming: The Twin Threats to American Democracy," *New York Times*, September 17, 2022. https://www.nytimes.com/2022/09/17/us/american-democracy-threats.html.

Richard Morrison, "Corporate 'Power' Is Limited and Temporary—Government Power Is the Real Threat," Competitive Enterprise Institute, June 6, 2019. https://cei.org/blog/corporate-power-is-limited-and-temporary-government-power-is-the-real-threat/.

Matt Pearce, "American Media Wants to Save Democracy. Is It Helping?" *Los Angeles Times*, July 29, 2022. https://www.latimes.com/entertainment-arts/story/2022-07-29/la-ent-american-media-democracy.

K. Sabeel Rahman, "Corporate Power and the Unmaking of American Democracy," *American Prospect*, May 16, 2018. https://prospect.org/infrastructure/corporate-power-unmaking-american-democracy/.

George F. Will, "Public Broadcasting's Immortality Defies Reason," *Washington Post*, June 2, 2017. https://www.washingtonpost.com/opinions/public-broadcastings-immortality-defies-reason/2017/06/02/f5de02be-46fe-11e7-a196-a1bb629f64cb_story.html.

OPPOSING VIEWPOINTS® SERIES

Chapter 3

# Does Corporate Influence Taint Medicine and Scientific Research?

## Chapter Preface

We like to think of science as pure and free from the constraints of commercial interests. But science is expensive. Someone has to pay for all that research. Government funding for science has been reduced over the years while the cost of completing scientific research has increased. That's left big business to fill in the gap and take on more of the share of paying for research. However, unlike pure scientific research, businesses have more at stake than simply finding out the truth or serving the public good. The goals of business are very different from the goals of science, and the two sets of goals do not always align well. Businesses are expected to make money for their shareholders. And all too often today, the companies funding the research are the companies that produce and profit from sales of the drugs being studied. This creates the temptation for private enterprise to corrupt scientific research for their own gain.

The authors in this chapter look at a variety of complexities, both moral and economic, that present themselves when corporations fund science. The first viewpoint looks at biomedical meta-analyses, a type of study intended to help busy doctors understand the body of research on a given issue without spending many hours they can't spare reading individual research papers. The author finds that the drug industry can turn this potentially useful shortcut into a useful tool for promoting their own drugs—whether or not those drugs are actually better than the other therapies being studied.

Another viewpoint argues that scientific research can be influenced by a variety of conflicts of interest, both subtle and blatant. Other viewpoints in this chapter address the problems of competition in the health care marketplace, risks to patients, the role of regulation in the health care industry, and the public's views on how much they trust corporate-funded scientific research.

Viewpoint 1

> *"The drug industry has started using meta-analysis for commercial purposes, rather than as a disinterested look at the evidence."*

# The Drug Industry Manipulates Scientific Research

*Richard Harris*

*Doctors depend on medical research to help them make decisions about treating their patients. In this viewpoint, Richard Harris points out that drug companies manipulate medical research to make their products seem more helpful or less risky than they actually are. When drug companies fund meta-analyses involving their own drugs, there is a clear conflict of interest, which brings the reliability of the meta-analysis into question. Richard Harris is a science correspondent of National Public Radio (NPR) and author of* Rigor Mortis: How Sloppy Science Creates Worthless Cures, Crushes Hope, and Wastes Billions.

As you read, consider the following questions:

1. According to this viewpoint, how can pharmaceutical companies use meta-analyses as marketing tools?

2. In this viewpoint, Harris quotes an expert saying that honest researchers can be biased as well. What examples does he give?
3. How does the use of meta-analyses make it easier for drug companies to manipulate medical research and mislead doctors?

When doctors want to help untangle confusing and sometimes contradictory findings in the scientific literature, they often turn to specially crafted summary studies. These are considered the gold standard for evidence. But one of the leading advocates for this practice is now raising alarm about them, because they are increasingly being tainted by commercial interests.

For many years, these studies—called meta-analyses and systematic reviews—seemed to solve a big problem. Doctors who had once relied on each other's expert opinions to select the best treatments gradually turned to careful scientific studies instead.

But the number of studies mushroomed and often came to different conclusions. So in the 1990s, doctors and medical advisory committees started relying on studies that combined results from many different research projects to streamline the search for answers.

These kinds of studies are "extremely important," says Dr. John Ioannidis, a professor of medicine health research and policy at Stanford University. He has conducted many of these types of studies over the course of his career. "They're trying to make some sense out of a very convoluted scientific and medical literature."

But Ioannidis says unfortunately things have gotten out of hand. First, "the problem is that there are just too many meta-analyses," Ioannidis says.

In a recent study on the subject, titled "The Mass Production of Redundant, Misleading, and Conflicted Systematic Reviews and Meta-Analyses," he chose as an example studies involving antidepressant drugs. "There are 185 of them published in the literature within seven years, which means about 25 of them published every year for the very same drugs and the very same indication, major depression," Ioannidis said.

What's worse, they're increasingly being generated by scientists who have financial interests in the outcome, Ioannidis found.

"About 80 percent of them have been funded or have some other conflicts of interest with manufacturers of these drugs," he says. "If you look at what their conclusions are, those that have been authored by industry employees, practically all of them, with one exception, have claimed that there are no caveats about antidepressants."

You have to read deep into the studies to find warnings about potential suicide risks, for example—if downsides are mentioned at all.

That's potentially misleading to doctors who turn to this kind of analysis to get a quick take on what works and what doesn't. Ioannidis says the drug industry has started using meta-analysis for commercial purposes, rather than as a disinterested look at the evidence.

"They can get the results or at least the interpretation that fits their needs. So you have the most powerful and most prestigious design in current medical evidence, and it can be easily manipulated as an advertisement, as a marketing tool."

And that defeats one of the main purposes of these studies, which is to make an overflowing scientific literature more manageable.

Peter Kramer, a clinical professor emeritus at Brown University and author of *Listening to Prozac*, took a deep dive into meta-analyses when he was writing his latest book, *Ordinarily Well*. He found the situation even worse than Ioannidis suggests.

"In some ways my doubts are stronger than his," Kramer told Shots.

Some analyses he looked at were trying to parse very subtle differences—for example, comparing two very similar antidepressants. You could get any answer you want, depending on how you set up the study, Kramer says.

And the problems he found aren't simply commercial conflicts of interest. For example, he saw biases among academics who were wedded to the notion that placebos are just as good as actual drugs for depression.

"Even on that side of the equation, where there's no adverse sponsorship but just an allegiance to an idea, I thought it wasn't always the case that everybody's hands were on the table," Kramer said.

But financial conflicts are easier to identify. Five years ago, the National Academy's Institute of Medicine (now called the National Academy of Medicine) suggested dozens of standards that should apply to systematic reviews of the research literature.

The influence of funders is a concern, says Dr. Alfred Berg, a professor emeritus of family medicine at the University of Washington who chaired one of the committees.

"If there's obvious sponsorship from an organization that might have a conflict of interest, that's probably not a good idea," he says. It's reasonable to suggest that scientists with clear financial conflicts of interest should not be producing these studies. "Is it going to happen in my lifetime?" Berg says. "Probably not!"

Pfizer, one of the many drug companies that fund meta-analyses involving their own products, declined an interview request. But the company noted in an emailed statement that the drug company "shares data from its clinical trials with outside members of the research community for them to conduct their own independent meta-analyses."

Fortunately, scientific journals are starting to do a better job of making sure researchers disclose their financial interests. It's up to readers now to take heed.

Viewpoint 2

*"There is now abundant evidence that the involvement of pharmaceutical companies corrupts medical science."*

# Corporate Corruption of Medical Science Is Deeper than Just Funding

*Sergio Sismondo*

*The previous viewpoint discussed the problem of pharmaceutical companies misleading doctors about scientific research. In this viewpoint, Sergio Sismondo examines the results of the loss of trust that comes when people can no longer trust sources of knowledge they once relied on. Though he is clear that studies funded by drug companies are biased, he argues that the problem is more complex than just funding. Studies funded by pharmaceutical companies make use of the methods and structures used in medical science to legitimize their research, finding ways to integrate their own research into medical science. Sergio Sismondo is a professor of philosophy at Queen's University, Canada.*

As you read, consider the following questions:

1. How does the author define "epistemic corruption"?
2. What are CROs and how does the use of them corrupt medical research?

"Epistemic Corruption, the Pharmaceutical Industry, and the Body of Medical Science," by Sergio Sismondo, Frontiers Media S.A., March 28, 2021. https://www.frontiersin.org/articles/10.3389/frma.2021.614013/full. 

3. According to Sismondo, how do pharmaceutical companies make their research look legitimate?

When a knowledge system importantly loses integrity, ceasing to provide the kinds of trusted knowledge expected of it, we can label this epistemic corruption. Epistemic corruption often occurs because the system has been co-opted for interests at odds with some of the central goals thought to lie behind it. There is now abundant evidence that the involvement of pharmaceutical companies corrupts medical science. Within the medical community, this is generally assumed to be the result of conflicts of interest. However, some important ways that the industry corrupts are not captured well by standard analyses in terms of conflicts of interest. It is not just that there is a body of medical science perverted by industry largesse. Instead, much of the corruption of medical science via the pharmaceutical industry happens through grafting activities: Pharmaceutical companies do their own research and smoothly integrate it with medical science, taking advantage of the legitimacy of the latter.

## Introduction: Epistemic Corruption

"Corrupt" and its cognates are old terms with many metaphorical uses. Bodies, fruits and meats are corrupted when they begin to rot, decompose, or otherwise spoil. What is thought pure is corrupted when mixed with something foul or lesser, as when air is made foul by pestilence or smoke, noble lineages are supposedly lessened by poor marriages, or people become less good simply because of the pressures of society. "Each of us is born with a share of purity, predestined to be corrupted by our commerce with mankind, by that sin against solitude" (Cioran 2012 [1949]).

It is only a small step from the introduction of pollution to the perversion of ends, as when a public official is corrupted by money or power for a purpose, to serve some interests rather than others. This is the most familiar kind of corruption today—so common that the metaphor has largely died—in which corrupted office holders and institutions have been captured by outside interests, or perhaps serve only their own interests. Thus there is a United Nations Convention against Corruption, which never needs to explicitly define "corruption," though it identifies it as involving a constellation of crimes that include bribery, embezzlement, influence peddling, illicit enrichment, etc., (United Nations 2004).

There can be value in analyzing knowledge systems in terms of all the above and other senses of the metaphor. When a knowledge system importantly loses integrity, ceasing to provide the kinds of trusted knowledge expected of it, or even in some cases when it ceases to establish trust, we can label this epistemic corruption. For example, the weaknesses of mathematical models can become entrenched, especially if they are constantly adjusted through curve-fitting, as has been claimed about several epidemiological models of the spread of Covid-19 (e.g., Jewell et al., 2020). Or, environmental toxicology may systematically lack information about the risks of a large number of industrial and agricultural chemicals, because powerful entities can control private science (e.g., on fluorinated compounds see Richter et al., 2018) and shape public science (e.g., on glyphosate, see Thacker 2019). And, outside the sciences, although many accusations of "fake news" are wide of the mark, large swaths of both social and traditional media are genuinely untrustworthy, whether because of interests that shape the creation or the dissemination of news, or because of inherent weaknesses of systems designed to capture audiences' attention.

My focus here is on how the pharmaceutical industry corrupts medical science. Using its very substantial resources, pharmaceutical companies co-opt medical knowledge systems for their particular interests, interests that conflict with the integrity and at least some of the central goals thought to lie behind medicine. It would seem that the body of medical science is corrupted because some assumed purity—though purity is always notional—has been affected by contact with outside interests.

## Pharmaceutical Industry Affects Medical Research

For the past 25 years, researchers have been studying the effects of industry funding—most often from pharmaceutical companies—on medical science. One typical protocol compares outcomes in industry-funded and other clinical trials in some therapeutic area, or for some class of drugs or medical devices, working either from searches of the published literature or from some other sample, such as conference abstracts. Most reports of clinical trials declare sources of funding, so analysts can often cleanly divide publications and make comparisons. In addition, clinical trials within areas often have enough uniformity that meta-analyses can sometimes be done. Since the mid-1990s, there have been hundreds of published studies of industry influence, comparing many thousands of clinical trials across all domains of medicine. The researchers designing and following these protocols often frame them as analogous to medical studies, with industry funding being the intervention, and the integrity and stability of the body of medical research being the outcome.

A 2017 *Cochrane Review* (Lundh et al., 2017, updated from; Lundh et al., 2012) provides a meta-analysis of such studies of industry funding, in which 75 studies, comparing more than 8,000 trials, met inclusion criteria. In all of its dimensions, the 2017 meta-analysis arrives at the same or similar results as had earlier quantitative and qualitative reviews (Bekelman et al., 2003; Lexchin et al., 2003; Schott et al., 2010). In the meta-analysis, industry funding had a risk ratio of 1.27 (95% CI: 1.17–1.51) of producing favorable efficacy results, and of 1.34 (95% CI: 1.19–1.51) of drawing favorable overall conclusions (in this study the harm results were not statistically different between industry and non-industry funding). Since there is no reason to think that non-industry funding skews results in any consistent direction, one can only conclude that industry funding biases the outcomes of clinical trials. Put simply, if a pharmaceutical company funds a trial, the chances of results and conclusions in that company's favor are increased. However, in this study, industry and non-industry research did not differ on such standard methodological quality concerns as sequence generation, allocation concealment, follow-up, or selective outcome reporting; and industry sponsored studies even had better blinding procedures.

The authors of the *Cochrane Review* conclude: "Our analyses suggest the existence of an industry bias that cannot be explained by standard 'Risk of bias' assessments" (Lundh et al., 2017). When pharmaceutical and other companies sponsor research there is a bias—a systematic tendency toward results serving their interests—but the bias is not seen in the formal factors routinely associated with low-quality science. The implication is that industry funding itself should be considered a standard "risk of bias" factor in clinical trials, one that is quantifiable, and even quantified, and pushes in predictable directions. Industry funding affects the results of clinical trials.

## But Funding Is Rarely Just Funding

The *Cochrane Review* I have just described shows that the pharmaceutical industry corruption of medical science doesn't happen through the mechanisms currently assessed by typical formal methodological measures. Funding itself corrupts medical science. But this does not mean that it is mysterious.

The most common way of understanding corruption through funding is in terms of conflict of interest. Perhaps funding and payments to researchers create conflicts of interest, which—for conscious or unconscious reasons—affect their actions, their judgments, and their conclusions. As a result, these conflicted researchers become more likely to report outcomes friendly to their funders. However, something else is at play here as well, and it is this that I want to illustrate below.

There is abundant evidence that conflicts of interest are important in many domains, including across medicine. For example, financial conflicts on committees producing clinical practice guidelines tend to produce assessments of evidence and recommendations that favor the companies and industries involved (Cosgrove et al., 2013; Lexchin 2020). In terms of medical practice, a recent systematic review shows that payments to physicians influence prescribing (Mitchell et al., 2020). The broad issue of conflict of interest is important enough that the United States Institute of Medicine issued a detailed report on it, overwhelmingly about how financial conflicts involving industry affect researchers' and physicians' judgment (Institute of Medicine, 2009). Despite such evidence, a focus on conflict of interest hides how pharmaceutical companies influence published results and outcomes.

Funding is rarely just funding. Most pharmaceutical company-sponsored clinical trials are designed, organized, audited, analyzed, and written up by the companies and their hired subcontractors. This is all work that happens behind the scenes, obscured by the form of academic publication. Thus much of the corruption can happen through more substantive medical choices and through structures of influence and control, as I describe below.

Roughly 70–75% of the industry's expenditures on clinical trials go to contract research organizations (CROs), rather than to independent researchers in the form of grants (Mirowski and Van Horn 2005; Fisher 2008; Westrock 2016). CROs together have revenue estimated to be approximately US$50 billion in 2020, most of it coming from pharmaceutical industry clinical trials (Fortune Business Insights, 2019). As a result, in the comparison of "industry-sponsored" and independent research, in most cases the "sponsorship" involves direct control over the research.

Even when it appears that industry-sponsored trials are led by academic or other actors, and that their subjects are recruited via independent clinics, hospitals and academic medical centers, it is most likely that at a higher level they are run by CROs working for pharmaceutical companies, and analyzed by company statisticians and others. Manuscripts are most likely drafted by ghostwriters on structures created by publication planners, and then shepherded through to publication by those planners, with limited opportunities for their academic and other independent authors to contribute (Fugh-Berman and Dodgson, 2008; Sismondo 2009; Matheson 2016). The published articles, then, are largely creations of the companies, even if the nominal authors include independent researchers. All of this constitutes the "ghost-management" of medical research (Sismondo 2018).

The ghost-management of trials affords many opportunities to intervene on individual publications and to affect the published record, producing the effects of industry sponsorship I described above. I list some significant categories, for each of which I provide an example or evidence.

(a) Companies can design studies that are likely to produce favorable results, making careful choices of comparators, doses, experimental populations, surrogate endpoints, trial durations, and definitions. For example, in Merck's testing of its COX-2 inhibitor rofecoxib, it used most of these techniques to improve one or another of its published trials (Whitstock 2018).

(b) Given the ghost-management of industry-funded research, funding almost certainly affects the interpretation of data and the writing of articles. Internal company documents and presentations show that the companies are fully aware of the opportunities for spin (e.g., Moffatt and Elliott 2007; McHenry 2010).

(c) Sometimes the corruption goes so far as to count as scientific misconduct, such as direct manipulation of data, omission of adverse events, etc. On the basis of documents from litigation against Forest Laboratories for misleading marketing of citalopram, Jureidini et al. (2016) establish conclusively that the ghost-management of the research allowed company employees to publish efficacy and safety conclusions that were inconsistent with what the trial data could support.

(d) Industry trials with positive results are over-represented in the medical journals, and those with negative results are under-represented, resulting in significant publication biases. In antidepressant trials submitted to regulatory agencies such as the United States Food and Drug Administration (Turner et al., 2008) or the Swedish regulatory agency (Melander et al., 2003)—and thus all industry trials—positive results are much more likely to be published. The positive trials are often multiply published by lumping and splitting, than are those with negative results. This has produced an impression in the medical literature that the evidence for the effectiveness of antidepressants is much stronger than it actually is.

(e) Industry trials are more cited than are non-industry trials (Gorry 2015). This may be because when publication planners assign a manuscript to a ghostwriter, it appears that a list of references is frequently one of the key inputs, and companies have good marketing reasons to cite themselves (Sismondo 2020). However, the higher level of citation may be simply a result of the fact that pharmaceutical companies have much better resources for promoting their own trials than individual researchers have. For example, the companies employ thousands upon thousands of "key opinion leaders" to give talks to physicians, using prepared slide shows, on recent clinical research (Moynihan 2008; Sismondo 2018).

The pharmaceutical industry corrupts medical science and the medical literature through these mechanisms and many more (Sismondo 2018). In the ghost-management of research, much of the corruption does not happen via traditionally conceived conflicts of interest of independent medical researchers. Instead, it happens by more direct actions by drug companies and their agents, such as those listed in (a) to (e) above.

## Discussion: The Body of Medical Science

While it initially seems likely that medical science is corrupted by medical researchers' conflicts of interest, that picture doesn't capture at least some of what is going on. Instead, pharmaceutical companies create their own research and their own ways of disseminating that research, relying on structures and traditions of medical science to legitimate their work. While we could talk of companies as having conflicts of interest, it is more natural to talk of them as acting in their own interests.

In the pharmaceutical companies' ghost-management of research, much of the corruption of medical science happens through a process of grafting. Grafts on plants make two bodies into one, typically allowing a fruiting part of a plant of value—to the horticulturist—to thrive by drawing on nutrients provided by a different plant's rootstock. Grafting involves a carefully constructed parasitic relationship. Similarly, pharmaceutical companies add substantially to medical science, doing their own research, smoothly attaching it to medical science in a way that integrates it, and then nurturing it to make it predominate. Non-industry medical science provides legitimacy to the apparently similar additions. The effects of industry sponsorship of medical research are the results of prominent additions to the body of medical science, not the simple introduction of an element—such as funding—that infects what it touches.

Of course, the pharmaceutical industry is a huge one, and in some areas of medicine the grafts permeate or overwhelm everything else in the area. And it is likely that the grafts affect the bodies onto which they are grafted: industry science may, for example, create costly research norms that in turn create demand for more industry funding.

Like most systems that can be corrupted, medical science has never been pure or perfect. But the pharmaceutical industry can trade on the presumed innocence of medical research's overriding goal: creating knowledge to benefit patient health. That is, some standard narratives of medical research attribute to it purity of heart, and a mere shortage of means that can be rectified by industry support.

In a very different context, Kierkegaard (1995: 76) writes: "As the world changes, the forms of corruption also gradually become more cunning, more difficult to point out." In its corruption of medical science, the pharmaceutical industry has borne this out.

## References

Bekelman, J. E., Li, Y., and Gross, C. P. (2003). Scope and impact of financial conflicts of interest in biomedical research: a systematic review. JAMA 289 (4), 454–465. doi:10.1001/jama.289.4.454

Institute of Medicine (2009). in Conflict of interest in medical research, education, and practice. Editors B. Lo, and M. J. Field (Washington, DC: National Academies Press). Available at: https://www.ncbi.nlm.nih.gov/books/NBK22942/pdf/Bookshelf_NBK22942.pdf (Accessed October 2, 2020).

Cioran, E. (2012). [1949] A short history of decay. Editor R. Howard (New York, NY: Arcade Publishing), 200.

Cosgrove, L., Bursztajn, H., Erlich, D., Wheeler, E. E., and Shaughnessy, A. F. (2013). Conflicts of interest and the quality of recommendations in clinical guidelines. J. Eval. Clin. Pract. 19, 674–681. doi:10.1111/jep.12016

Fisher, J. A. (2008). Medical research for hire: the political economy of pharmaceutical clinical trials. New Brunswick, NJ: Rutgers University Press, 272.

Fortune Business Insights (2019). Contract research organization (CRO) services market. Available at: https://www.fortunebusinessinsights.com/industry-reports/contract-research-organization-cro-services-market-100864 (Accessed October 2, 2020).

Fugh Berman, A., and Dodgson, S. J. (2008). Ethical considerations of publication planning in the pharmaceutical industry. Open Med. 2 (4), e121–e124.

Gorry, P. (2015). Medical literature imprinting by Pharma ghost writing: a scientometric evaluation. Proceedings of ISSI 2015 Istanbul: 650–651. Available at: https://www.issi-society.org/proceedings/issi_2015/0650.pdf (Accessed February 23, 2021).

Jewell, N. P., Lewnard, J. A., and Jewell, B. L. (2020). Caution warranted: using the Institute for health Metrics and evaluation model for predicting the course of the COVID-19 pandemic. Ann. Intern. Med. 173, 226–227. doi:10.7326/M20-1565

Jureidini, J. N., Amsterdam, J. D., and McHenry, L. B. (2016). The citalopram CIT-MD-18 pediatric depression trial: deconstruction of medical ghostwriting, data mischaracterisation and academic malfeasance. Int. J. Risk Saf. Med. 28 (1), 33–43. doi:10.3233/JRS-160671

Kierkegaard, S. (1995). Works of love: Kierkegaard's writings. Editors H. V. Hong, and E. H. Hong (Princeton, NJ: Princeton University Press), Vol. 16.

Lexchin, J., Bero, L. A., Djulbegovic, B., and Clark, O. (2003). Pharmaceutical industry sponsorship and research outcome and quality: systematic review. BMJ 326 (7400), 1167–1170. doi:10.1136/bmj.326.7400.1167

Lexchin, J. (2020). Clinical practice guidelines and managing financial conflicts of interest. eLS 1 (2), 263–269. doi:10.1002/9780470015902.a0029129

Lundh, A., Lexchin, J., Mintzes, B., Schroll, J. B., and Bero, L. (2017). Industry sponsorship and research outcome. Cochrane Database Syst. Rev. 2, MR000033. doi:10.1002/14651858.MR000033.pub3

Lundh, A., Sismondo, S., Lexchin, J., Busuioc, O. A., and Bero, L. (2012). Industry sponsorship and research outcome. Cochrane Database Syst. Rev. 12, MR000033. doi:10.1002/14651858.MR000033.pub2

Matheson, A. (2016). Ghostwriting: the importance of definition and its place in contemporary drug marketing. BMJ 354, i4578. doi:10.1136/bmj.i4578

McHenry, L. (2010). Of sophists and spin-doctors: industry-sponsored ghostwriting and the crisis of academic medicine. Mens Sana Monogr. 8 (1), 129–145. doi:10.4103/0973-1229.58824

Melander, H., Ahlqvist-Rastad, J., Meijer, G., and Beermann, B. (2003). Evidenced b(i) ased medicine—selective reporting from studies sponsored by pharmaceutical industry: review of studies in new drug applications. BMJ 326, 1171–1173. doi:10.1136/bmj.326.7400.1171

Mirowski, P., and Van Horn, R. (2005). The contract research organization and the commercialization of scientific research. Soc. Stud. Sci. 35 (4), 503–548. doi:10.1177/0306312705052103

Mitchell, A. P., Trivedi, N. U., and Gennarelli, R. L. (2020). Are financial payments from the pharmaceutical industry associated with physician prescribing? a systematic review. Ann. Intern. Med. [Epub ahead of print]. doi:10.7326/M20-5665

Moffatt, B., and Elliott, C. (2007). Ghost marketing: pharmaceutical companies and ghostwritten journal articles. Perspect. Biol. Med. 50, 18–31. doi:10.1353/pbm.2007.0009

Moynihan, R. (2008). Key opinion leaders: independent experts or drug representatives in disguise?. BMJ 336 (7658), 1402–1403. doi:10.1136/bmj.39575.675787.651

Richter, L., Cordner, A., and Brown, P. (2018). Non-stick science: sixty years of research and (in)action on fluorinated compounds. Soc. Stud. Sci. 48 (5), 691–714. doi:10.1177/0306312718799960

Schott, G., Pachl, H., Limbach, U., Gundert-Remy, U., Ludwig, W. D., and Lieb, K. (2010). The financing of drug trials by pharmaceutical companies and its consequences, part 1: a qualitative, systematic review of the literature on possible influences on the findings, protocols, and quality of drug trials. Dtsch. Arztebl. Int. 107 (16), 279. doi:10.3238/arztebl.2010.0279

Sismondo, S. (2018). Ghost-managed medicine: big pharma's invisible hands. Manchester, United Kingdom: Mattering Press, 234.

Sismondo, S. (2020). "Ghost-managing and gaming pharmaceutical knowledge," in Gaming the metrics: misconduct and manipulation in academic research. Editors M. Biagioli, and A. Lippman (Cambridge, MA: MIT Press), 123–134.

Sismondo, S. (2009). Ghosts in the machine: publication planning in the medical sciences. Soc. Stud. Sci. 39 (2), 171–198. doi:10.1177/0306312708101047

Thacker, P. D. (2019). An inside look at how Monsanto, a PR firm and a reporter give readers a warped view of science. Available at: https://www.huffpost.com/entry/monsanto-public-relations-reporter-warped-science-view_n_5d485c14e4b0ca604e3636b5?11&fbclid=IwAR3nyp4iCmHdnEYhBpyiLvAfqkreTkCGSlqEqJKEazLXPbWCPyFXXl2d3nU (Accessed August 13, 2019).

Turner, E. H., Matthews, A. M., Linardatos, E., Tell, R. A., and Rosenthal, R. (2008). Selective publication of antidepressant trials and its influence on apparent efficacy. NEJM 358, 252–260. doi:10.1056/NEJMsa065779

United Nations (2004). United Nation convention against corruption. New York, NY: United NationsAvailable at: https://www.unodc.org/unodc/en/corruption/tools_and_publications/UN-convention-against-corruption.html (Accessed October 2, 2020).

Westrock (2016). Patient-centric clinical trial solutions: adherence, outcomes and data. Available at: https://pages.questexweb.com/WestRock-20160524-Registration.html (Accessed May 15, 2016).

Whitstock, M. (2018). Manufacturing the truth: from designing clinical trials to publishing trial data. Indian J. Med. Ethics 3, 152–153. doi:10.20529/IJME.2017.096

Viewpoint 3

> *"The pharmaceutical, chemical, nutrition and petroleum industries have all weathered criticism of their research integrity, and for good reason."*

# The Public Doesn't Trust Scientific Research When Companies Are Involved

*John C. Besley, Aaron M. McCright, Joseph D. Martin, Kevin Elliot, and Nagwan Zahry*

*The previous two viewpoints explored various ways corporate interests corrupt medical research. In this viewpoint, the authors explore how the public feels about that—whether in medicine or other areas of science. They argue that the public's attitude toward corporate influence over research might apply to good research as well as bad. John C. Besley, Aaron M. McCright, and Kevin Elliot are professors at Michigan State University. Joseph D. Martin is a fellow-in-residence at the University of Leeds, and at the time this viewpoint was written, Nagwan Zahry was a PhD student at the University of Michigan.*

"People Don't Trust Scientific Research When Companies Are Involved," by John C. Besley, Aaron M. McCright, Joseph D. Martin, Kevin Elliot, and Nagwan Zahry, The Conversation, May 8, 2017. https://theconversation.com/people-dont-trust-scientific-research-when-companies-are-involved-76848. 

As you read, consider the following questions:

1. According to this viewpoint, what are the downsides of public distrust of industry involvement in science?
2. How do the authors suggest overcoming the downsides of public distrust of industry involvement?
3. According to these authors, how has public perception of industry changed in the last few decades?

A soda company sponsoring nutrition research. An oil conglomerate helping fund a climate-related research meeting. Does the public care who's paying for science?

In a word, yes. When industry funds science, credibility suffers. And this does not bode well for the types of public-private research partnerships that appear to be becoming more prevalent as government funding for research and development lags.

The recurring topic of conflict of interest has made headlines in recent weeks. The National Academies of Science, Engineering, and Medicine has revised its conflict of interest guidelines following questions about whether members of a recent expert panel on GMOs had industry ties or other financial conflicts that were not disclosed in the panel's final report.

Our own recent research speaks to how hard it may be for the public to see research as useful when produced with an industry partner, even when that company is just one of several collaborators.

## What People Think of Funding Sources

We asked our study volunteers what they thought about a proposed research partnership to study the potential risks related to either genetically modified foods or trans fats.

We randomly assigned participants to each evaluate one of 15 different research partnership arrangements—various combinations of scientists from a university, a government agency, a nongovernmental organization and a large food company.

For example, 1/15th of participants were asked to consider a research collaboration that included only university researchers. Another 1/15th of participants considered a research partnership that included both university and government scientists, and so on. In total we presented four conditions where there was a single type of researcher, another six collaborations with two partners, four with three partners and one with all four partners.

When a research team included an industry partner, our participants were generally less likely to think the scientists would consider a full range of evidence and listen to different voices. An industry partner also reduced how much participants believed any resulting data would provide meaningful guidance for making decisions.

At the outset of our work, we thought including a diverse array of partners in a research collaboration might mitigate the negative perceptions that come with industry involvement. But, while including scientists from a nonindustry organization (particularly a nongovernmental organization) made some difference, the effect was small. Adding a government partner provided no substantive additional benefit.

When we asked participants to describe what they thought about the research partnership in their own words, they were skeptical whether an industry partner could ever be trusted to release information that might hurt its profits.

Our results may be even more troubling because we chose a company with a good reputation. We used pretests to select particular examples—of a corporation, as well as a university, government agency and nongovernmental organization—that had relatively high positive ratings and relatively low negative ratings in a test sample.

## Can Industry Do Valid Science?

You don't have to look far for real-life examples of poorly conducted or intentionally misleading industry research. The pharmaceutical, chemical, nutrition and petroleum industries have all weathered criticism of their research integrity, and for good reason. These ethically questionable episodes no doubt fuel public skepticism of industry research. Stories of pharmaceutical companies conducting less than rigorous clinical trials for the benefit of their marketing departments, or the tobacco industry steadfastly denying the connection between smoking and cancer in the face of mounting evidence, help explain public concern about industry-funded science.

But industry generally has a long and impressive history of supporting scientific research and technical development. Industry-supported research has generated widely adopted technologies, driven the evolution of entire economic sectors, improved processes that were harmful to public health and the environment and won Nobel Prizes. And as scientists not currently affiliated with industry scramble to fund their research in an era of tight budgets, big companies have money to underwrite science.

Can this lack of trust be overcome? Moving forward, it will be essential to address incentives such as short-term profit or individual recognition that can encourage poor research—in any institutional context. By showing how quickly people may judge industry-funded research, our work indicates that it's critical to think about how the results of that research can be communicated effectively.

Our results should worry those who want research to be evaluated largely on its scientific merits, rather than based upon the affiliations of those involved.

Although relatively little previous scholarship has investigated this topic, we expected to find that including multiple, nonindustry organizations in a scientific partnership might, at least partly, assuage participants' concerns about industry involvement. This reflects our initial tentative belief that, given the resources and expertise within industry, there must be some way to create public-private partnerships that produce high-quality research which is perceived widely as such.

Our interdisciplinary team—a risk communication scholar, a sociologist, a philosopher of science, a historian of science and a toxicologist—is also examining philosophical arguments and historical precedents for guidance on these issues.

Philosophy can tell us a great deal about how the values of investigators can influence their results. And history shows that not so long ago, up until a few decades after World War II, many considered industry support a way to uphold research integrity by protecting it from government secrecy regimes.

Looking forward, we are planning additional social scientific experiments to examine how specific procedures that research partnerships sometimes use may affect public views about collaborations with industry partners. For example, perhaps open-data policies, transparency initiatives or external reviewer processes may alleviate bias concerns.

Given the central role that industry plays in scientific research and development, it is important to explore strategies for designing multi-sector research collaborations that can generate legitimate, high-quality results while being perceived as legitimate by the public.

VIEWPOINT 4

> *"Performance incentives (mostly volumes without quality), covert bribes from suppliers, research temptations, etc., become daily threats to medical ethics and morality."*

# When Health Care Is a Business, Patients Can Suffer at the Expense of Revenue

*Teodora Elena Ucenic*

*After several viewpoints on the corporatization of scientific research, this viewpoint turns to the corporatization of the delivery of health care. In this viewpoint, Teodora Elena Ucenic explains different models of funding health care, in what parts of the world these models are used, and how they protect (or do not protect) patients and physicians. Models that create a privatized health care industry that is controlled by industry rather than the government offer fewer protections for patients and doctors alike. Teodora Elena Ucenic is a physician at NMC Specialty Hospital in Al Ain, United Arab Emirates.*

As you read, consider the following questions:

"When Healthcare Becomes a Business Who Do We Protect First: Patient or Revenue?" by Dr. Teodora Elena Ucenic, Omnia Health, January 6, 2020. Reprinted by permission.

1. According to this viewpoint, how can pressure to make money for health care organizations make it difficult for doctors to do their jobs ethically and effectively?
2. Why is the National Health Insurance Model cheaper and simpler to administrate?
3. Ucenic points out that despite having an "obsession" with productivity, the United States ranks low in health care quality and high in terms of spending. Why do you think this is the case?

Everybody knows healthcare is expensive. And as science and technology continue to advance, medical devices and treatments are becoming more sophisticated and certainly more expensive. Even more, the costs are naturally and artificially increasing in order to cover not only the medical service per se but also medical education, research, pharmaceutical industry profits, luxurious hospital buildings, etc. The last addition to the medical cost is the insurance industry profits. Worldwide, healthcare spending is increasing but the rate is very much different and not necessarily reflected in the quality of care or population health status.

For the relation between patient and doctor to even exist, few more additions are necessary e.g. nurses, laboratory, pharmacy and auxiliary services, such as cleaning, laundry, catering, safe/protection, IT, maintenance, etc.

The more complex the structures are, the larger the managerial team, including HR, marketing, quality control, and so on and so forth, will be. All these are built and sustained by patient-doctor binomial.

From the financial point of view, a healthcare entity can be categorised as either non-profit (generally administered by government) or profit making (typically private). While the non-profit hospitals largely accept and treat all ranges of age/social/

pathology and diversity of patients, the profit-making hospitals have the tendency to treat selected population groups.

While the non-profit hospitals—under the umbrella of national plans—concentrate to reduce costs and maximise population health, the profit-making hospitals focus on reducing costs and maximising profits. Even so, the difference in the strategic targets should not impact the quality of clinical care.

In many EU countries, strict laws and regulations ensure that profit healthcare organisations are not a threat for medical ethics, traditional mission and values of healthcare, and the autonomy and ideals of the medical profession.

## So, Who Is Paying?

There are more than 200 countries on our planet and each struggle with its own healthcare problems and cost cover. In some countries the burden is shared between the patient and the government in different scales of participation. In others, the patients cover all treatment costs through lifetime instalments paid through taxes or insurance companies, or ad-hoc at the point of service.

Generally, there are four systems which are applied with some local variations:

## The Beveridge Model

It is named after William Beveridge, the social reformer who designed Britain's National Health Service (NHS). In this system, healthcare is provided and financed by the government through tax payments, just like the police force.

Many, but not all, hospitals are owned by the government. In Britain, you never get a doctor's bill. These systems tend to have low costs per capita, because the government, as the sole payer, controls what doctors can do and what they can charge.

Countries using the Beveridge plan or variations of it include Great Britain, Spain, most of Scandinavia, New Zealand and Hong

Kong. Cuba represents the extreme application of the Beveridge approach; it is probably the world's purest example of total government control.

## The Bismarck Model

It is named after Prussian Chancellor Otto von Bismarck, who invented the welfare state as part of the unification of Germany in the 19th century. This system uses an insurance system—the insurers are called "sickness funds"—usually financed jointly by employers and employees through payroll deduction.

Bismarck-type health insurance plans have to cover everybody, and they don't make a profit. Doctors and hospitals tend to be private, but tight regulation gives government much of the cost-control clout similar to the single-payer Beveridge Model. The Bismarck model is found in Germany, France, Belgium, Netherlands, Japan, Switzerland, and, to a degree, in Latin America.

## The National Health Insurance Model (NHI)

This system has elements of both Beveridge and Bismarck. It uses private-sector providers, but payment comes from a government-run insurance programme that every citizen pays into. Since there's no need for marketing, no financial motive to deny claims and no profit, these universal insurance programmes tend to be cheaper and much simpler administratively than American-style for-profit insurance. The single payer tends to have considerable market power to negotiate for lower prices. The classic NHI system is found in Canada, with variants in Taiwan and South Korea.

## The Out-of-Pocket Model

Only the developed, industrialised countries—perhaps 40 of the world's 200 countries—have established healthcare systems.

This model applies to most of the nations that are too poor and too disorganised to provide any kind of mass medical care.

The basic rule in such countries is that the rich get medical care; the poor stay sick, die, or have some medical care depending on urgency and ability to afford.

## Where Does the Doctor Stand?

The intellectual, emotional, and psychological challenges a doctor faces day-by-day are extremely complex. Medical decision is one of the most intense brain processes, involving memory, situational analysis, perceptions, emotions and sometimes instincts, not to mention that this exercise is done multiple times in a day in an expected empathic way. There are in addition education, teaching, coaching and leading/managerial activities. New applied technologies require one of the fastest professional adaptation.

This is a profession where quality is demanded to the highest and there is no place for error or second chance. Historically, the doctor-patient relationship was built on equal trust and need. A doctor had a large grade of independence and his/her name or reputation was mostly based on clinical results, ethical behaviour and community recognition.

As societies developed, the health systems changed gradually to an extent where the doctor become a crushed layer between the patients and the medical organisations.

While the patient is interested to have the best possible care provided at the lowest possible cost, the organisation is interested to have the lowest possible costs for the unit of care. Even a non-profit organisation wants to be on a positive financial balance. When the hospital is a profit-making organisation, the financial pressure is significantly higher.

The doctor is faced with a dilemma of being a patient advocate but at the same time needing to respect and represent the hospital interests. Although intermediary structures were created to ease medical reporting and deal with the revenue, they are rarely appropriately and adequately staffed or have enough expertise. They usually have limited decision making authority and ultimately refer all problematic cases back to doctors.

To make things worse, financial temptations often challenge the ethical balance. Performance incentives (mostly volumes without quality), covert bribes from suppliers, research temptations, etc., become daily threats to medical ethics and morality.

## How Is a Patient Protected?

Over time, various mechanisms were created to safeguard the patient during the tenure of medical care. They are all oriented towards medical units headed by doctors. Each hospital, each national policy maker or administrator, produce an impressive amount of quality checks and indicators to protect the patient once medical care has been initiated. Loss of health due to medical error is amply analysed, and ultimately, guilty or not, doctors usually face the blame.

There is no tool to evaluate or ensure quality of medical care when there is no actual treatment offered. This means nobody can protect the patient against barriers in accessing medical help. Unaffordable medical care or refusal of treatment from insurance companies make far more victims than medical errors; and no one quantifies this.

## How Are Hospitals Ensuring Revenue Protection?

Both non-profit and profit, hospitals aim for a positive financial balance. Various services, internal or commissioned, were put in place to ensure this task. The more sophisticated and competent the service, the higher costs for operation. Mind that this operational price is paid by the doctor's service, which the doctor will afterwards be scrutinised on for productivity.

Positive and negative incentives were created in order to stimulate doctors to work hard. Enforcing volumes before quality typically increases income but is detrimental to clinical accuracy and evidence based best practice.

Whenever a profit insurance company is collaborating with a profit hospital and either of them has an unusual high revenue, there will be a large element of suspicion and distrust.

## Who Is Protecting the Doctors?

Interestingly, in spite of having minimal or no quantitative targets for doctors in public sector and self-imposed plans in private sector, the majority of European countries own the most developed health systems (WHO Report 2000, 21 among first 25 are European). The U.S., where the productivity obsession applies, occupies the 37th position worldwide while having the highest spending.

In the majority of European countries there are professional organisations (physician colleges or councils) that are authorised to judge medical errors. They are independent, and their expert decision cannot be overruled by individual hospitals, Ministry of Health or court. Unless intentional crime is proven, a doctor cannot be judged under criminal laws.

These are also countries where physicians feel most secure and protected. In the U.S., in case of medical liability, the hospital's defence strategy may or may not include a doctor, depending on financial loss. Reloading the initial question, the answer should be simple, but it is not. It is therefore fair to say that every system has and may use enough tools to encourage and protect doctors in making the right decision.

Viewpoint 5

> *"Health plan consolidation can have both positive and negative impacts, and appropriate regulation can enhance the positive while mitigating the negative."*

# Health Care Markets Need Just the Right Amount of Regulation

*Stuart Guterman*

*In this viewpoint, Stuart Guterman points out the potential advantages and disadvantages of regulating the health plan market and argues that too much regulation can stifle competition, but too little can harm both consumers and the system itself. Some regulation can help the health care market produce desired outcomes, but too much regulation can limit the amount and mix of health care resources that are available. The market structure for health care has to be balanced to allow for care that is high quality and low cost. Stuart Guterman is an economist and independent consultant to the health care industry.*

As you read, consider the following questions:

1. How does Guterman use basketball as an analogy for the proper amount of regulation?

"Making Health Care Markets Work Better: The Role of Regulation," by Stuart Guterman, the Commonwealth Fund, January 24, 2017. Reprinted by permission.

2. Why is competition essential in the health plan market, according to Guterman?
3. What are the pros and cons of health plan consolidation listed in this viewpoint?

For the past several years we've been hearing about mergers and consolidations in the health care industry, prompting concern about threats to competition in health care markets. While antitrust actions to promote competition are important, they are not enough to ensure we control health care costs and ensure quality. To enable market forces to work properly, we need to address flaws in the structure of the health care markets in which those forces operate. Although it may run counter to the emphasis on deregulation in the current political climate, well-chosen regulation may be necessary to make markets work better, and to avoid the need for more—and more onerous—regulations to counter the adverse results produced by a broken health care market structure.

## Threats to Competition

Competition is essential to ensure that providers and health plans are subject to the market forces that drive them to attract patients and subscribers by offering low prices and high quality. If market power is concentrated among providers or plans, they are insulated from those forces.

Threats to competition can be seen in both the health care provider and health plan markets. On the provider side, the push for greater coordination of care across settings, represented most prominently by the creation of accountable care organizations in the Affordable Care Act (ACA), has raised fears that hospitals and physicians, in the name of better coordination, will consolidate to increase their market power. Mergers and acquisitions among health care providers have indeed boomed in recent years, and federal authorities have taken action to block such activity when it is found to be deleterious to competition and consumer welfare.

Historically, increased consolidation among providers has been associated with higher prices and lower quality. But the current emphasis on moving from paying for the volume of services to paying for the value they produce may change that dynamic. In the context of these changing incentives—and with appropriate regulation—collaboration among providers could become a vehicle for producing more coordinated care and lower costs.

While provider consolidation tends to receive more attention, threats to competition among health plans have made headlines recently, with the Justice Department filing suit to stop proposed mergers between Aetna and Humana and between Anthem and Cigna. But health plan markets already are highly concentrated: in 2013, the nationwide average share of privately insured enrollees for the three largest insurers at the state level was 85 percent to 87 percent across the individual, small-group, and large-group markets.

Health plan consolidation can have both positive and negative impacts, and appropriate regulation can enhance the positive while mitigating the negative. On one hand, the market power of health plans in negotiating with providers could be a tool to counter consolidation in hospital markets, and it does appear to be correlated with lower provider prices. But health plan consolidation does not appear to produce lower premiums, as insurers can use their market power to continue to negotiate high premiums from employers. Actions to restrict the expansion of plans' market power can help in this regard, but additional regulation may be required.

## Market Forces and Market Structure

The market is the structure in which market forces operate; if that structure is operating properly, market forces can do their job to keep prices low and quality high. But if the market structure itself is flawed, market forces may not by themselves produce the desired results—in fact, they may do the opposite.

There are several conditions necessary for markets to function properly. Markets need more than a large number of buyers and sellers; there also must be information available about a product's quality and effectiveness, and a product's benefits and costs should be restricted to the consumer, among other conditions. In health care markets none of those conditions is met. Antitrust policy addresses only the need for a large number of buyers and sellers, and it does so incompletely.

## Using Regulation to Help Market Mechanisms Work Better

Regulation can help make health care market forces work better to produce the outcomes we desire. The key is to find the right balance: too much regulation, or the wrong kind, can impede the

### The ACA Put a Dent in the Health Care Cost Curve

A decade after the passage of the Patient Protection and Affordable Care Act of 2010, there is evidence that the landmark health legislation has contributed to slower growth in U.S. health care spending.

An analysis published in the March issue of the journal *Health Affairs* coincides with the 10-year anniversary of the law's passage and illustrates how the law has impacted health care spending, which currently consumes nearly one-fifth the entire gross domestic product in the U.S.

"It's clear that a number of the provisions in the ACA have dampened cost growth," said lead author Melinda Buntin, PhD, Mike Curb professor of health policy and chair of the Department of Health Policy at Vanderbilt University School of Medicine. "What remains to be seen is whether there is the will to continue these measures."

The analysis examines key policy reforms included in the ACA, including Medicaid insurance coverage expansion, Medicare payment reforms and reforms of private insurance markets. There have been broad studies and estimates about the law's effect on health care expenditures nationally but few definitive sources related to health spending since 2010.

ability of market forces to do the heavy lifting in determining the amount, mix, and distribution of health care resources; too little, on the other hand, can produce equally adverse results.

I'm reminded of an old radio interview that I read about with James Naismith, the inventor of basketball—a game admired for its free-flowing action and the degree to which it rewards creativity. In the interview, he described how the first attempt to play the game deteriorated into a "free-for-all in the middle of the gym floor." He decided what was needed was a set of rules, to ensure appropriate behavior in the context of extremely competitive circumstances.

So it is with health care (and all) markets: some regulation—such as review of proposed mergers—is necessary both to preserve

"While the ACA has made a dent, what also stands out to us is that further actions will be required in all sectors and at multiple levels of government to maintain the relatively slow rates of growth we have seen since passage of the ACA," Graves said.

The greatest savings, however, may be due to value-based payment initiatives, which aim to create incentives for physicians and hospitals to deliver high-quality care while keeping costs in check.

"In our opinion, the increased attention paid to value-based payment by non-Medicare payers—namely states and private insurers—is likely a key contributor to the slower rate of per capita cost growth that we've seen over the past decade," the study said.

"Disentangling the exact effects of a major piece of legislation from underlying trends is nearly impossible, but it is also nearly impossible to deny that the ACA has had far-reaching cost effects on the entire health care industry," Buntin and Graves wrote. "The most politically salient examples of high health care costs—including those due to the introduction of new drugs and out-of-network billing—are virtually unrelated to the ACA, while cost growth for health services in Medicare, Medicaid, and even Marketplace plans seems to be settling into a 'new normal' slower rate."

**"How the ACA Dented the Health Care Cost Curve," Vanderbilt University Medical Center, March 2, 2020.**

competition and to enforce the rules of the market. Preserving competition is critical to allowing market forces to function effectively, but the integrity of the market structure within which those forces operate must be protected by rules that ensure that it does not deteriorate into Naismith's "free-for-all in the middle of the gym floor"—or, worse yet, only one player left standing. Without those rules, markets by themselves will not produce the results we want or the health care system we need.

## Notes

1. R. H. Leftwich, The Price System and Resource Allocation (Holt, Rinehart and Winston, 1964).

## Periodical and Internet Sources Bibliography

*The following articles have been selected to supplement the diverse views presented in this chapter.*


Peter S. Arno and Philip Caper, "Medicare for All: Transformation of US Health Care," *Health Affairs*, March 25, 2020. https://www.healthaffairs.org/do/10.1377/forefront.20200319.920962/.

Richard G. Frank and Kathleen Hannick, "Five Things to Understand about Pharmaceutical R&D," Brookings Institution, June 2, 2022. https://www.brookings.edu/blog/usc-brookings-schaeffer-on-health-policy/2022/06/02/five-things-to-understand-about-pharmaceutical-rd/.

Paul Hsieh, "Does Your Doctor Work for a Private Equity Company —and Should You Care?" *Forbes*, January 31, 2022. https://www.forbes.com/sites/paulhsieh/2022/01/31/does-your-doctor-work-for-a-private-equity-company---and-should-you-care/?sh=2b7db906397a.

Stephen Moore, "Eight Reasons to Still Hate Obamacare," Heritage Foundation, June 5, 2018. https://www.heritage.org/health-care-reform/commentary/8-reasons-still-hate-obamacare.

Charles Piller and Jia You, "Hidden Conflicts? Pharma Payments to FDA Advisors After Drug Approvals Spark Ethical Concerns," *Science*, July 5, 2018. https://www.science.org/content/article/hidden-conflicts-pharma-payments-fda-advisers-after-drug-approvals-spark-ethical.

Naeem Rahman, "Here's What the Corporatization of Medicine is Doing," KevinMD, December 2018. https://www.kevinmd.com/2018/12/heres-what-the-corporatization-of-medicine-is-doing.html.

Nicole Rapfogel, Maura Calsyn, and Emily Gee, "Ten Ways the ACA Has Improved Health Care in the Past Decade," *American Progress,* March 23, 2020. *https:*//www.americanprogress.org/article/10-ways-aca-improved-health-care-past-decade/.

Erik Robinson, "Study Raises Red Flags About Corporatization of Health Care, OSHU Investigator Says," Oregon Health & Science University News, September 2, 2022. https://news.ohsu.

edu/2022/09/02/study-raises-red-flags-about-corporatization-of-health-care-ohsu-investigator-says.

Laura Spinney, "Drugs, Money, and Misleading Evidence," *Nature*, June 29, 2020. https://www.nature.com/articles/d41586-020-01911-7.

C. Michael White, "Why Is the FDA Funded in Part by the Companies It Regulates?" *UConn Today*, May 21, 2021. https://today.uconn.edu/2021/05/why-is-the-fda-funded-in-part-by-the-companies-it-regulates-2/.

OPPOSING VIEWPOINTS® SERIES

Chapter 4

# Do Tech Companies Have Too Much Power?

## Chapter Preface

Once it was railroads, then it was oil companies. Today the biggest and most powerful corporations are technology companies. Specifically Google, Facebook (now Meta), Amazon, and Apple. But these companies are even bigger and far more powerful than other companies have been in the past. They are also much more ingrained into the everyday lives of the people who use them. Add that to an outsized influence on government and you have a recipe for complications and controversy.

In this chapter, a variety of authors ask if big tech companies have too much power. If they do, what should (and shouldn't) be done about it?

The conversation considers the owners of big tech companies—specifically their tendency towards philanthropy. Is that a good thing? Should citizens be dependent on the largess of billionaires for the basics of life? Considering the political climate and the ever-increasing tendency to cut government spending, we may not have a choice, one author argues.

The rampant spread of false and/or misleading information is another problem posed by big tech. Authors here examine the issue and suggest some solutions. One argues that the public needs to become more media savvy and schools should teach media literacy.

Lastly, a viewpoint explores the question of rights. How does the first amendment's protection of speech apply to social media? Do the social media companies themselves have a right to control what is communicated on their platforms? Do they have a responsibility to keep it in check? This chapter examines the question of the role tech companies have in democracy and what powers they should and should not have over it.

Viewpoint 1

> *"Today, as thousands die and millions fall through a frayed social safety net, it's clearer than ever that America would be better off with higher taxes on the wealthy, a more robust government, and less reliance on charitable giving to solve problems."*

# Americans Shouldn't Be Dependent on the Generosity of the Wealthy, but the Need for Big Philanthropy Is Here to Stay

*David Callahan*

*Monopolies aren't the only way big tech influences control over society. Their billionaire owners are often philanthropists doing good—and influencing policy—with their money. However, David Callahan points out that if big corporations had not used their money and influence to reduce the power of government and funding for the social safety net, ordinary citizens wouldn't be dependent on the kindness of the wealthy to face crises like the COVID-19 pandemic. Unfortunately, Callahan argues, it is unlikely that the need for philanthropy will dissipate anytime soon. David Callahan is an author and founder of Inside Philanthropy.*

"Stronger Government Is a Must. But Billionaire Donors Are Here to Stay—and Can Do Good," by David Callahan, Inside Philanthropy, April 21, 2020. Reprinted by permission.

As you read, consider the following questions:

1. According to this viewpoint, how did the COVID-19 pandemic reveal the harms done by decades-long efforts to downsize government, reduce taxes on corporations, and gut the safety net?
2. According to Callahan, why would reducing the wealth at the top of society not eliminate the need for philanthropy?
3. According to this viewpoint, how do the wealthy influence government policy?

As billionaire donors have opened up their checkbooks in response to the coronavirus pandemic, it's hard to forget that the upper class is partly to blame for the fact that we don't have a stronger government at a moment of crisis.

Starting in the 1970s, wealthy philanthropists and foundations, along with business interests, waged a sweeping attack on government, looking to downsize federal agencies, gut the social safety net, and lower taxes—especially on the rich and corporations. The donor class also pumped billions into electing conservative politicians who've been dismissive of expertise and have attacked the public servants who populate public agencies.

COVID-19 is now shining a spotlight on this handiwork. In the face of a viral threat and mounting human suffering, the U.S. doesn't have the government it needs to cope with either a once-in-a-century public health crisis or an unprecedented economic meltdown. That didn't happen by accident, although the upper class is by no means solely to blame. Starting in the 1960s, white voters fled the Democratic Party in droves as it harnessed the power of government to extend new benefits to non-whites. The GOP has drawn substantial public support ever since for swinging a wrecking ball at the public sector.

But wealthy interests have played an outsized role in the campaign to bring down government, so it's no wonder that not everyone is applauding as a handful of billionaires like Bill Gates,

Jeff Bezos and Michael Dell make big donations in response to the pandemic. Instead, this crisis is putting an exclamation point on a critique that had already been gaining currency in recent years—that private philanthropists have too much money and power, while government has too little.

Today, as thousands die and millions fall through a frayed social safety net, it's clearer than ever that America would be better off with higher taxes on the wealthy, a more robust government, and less reliance on charitable giving to solve problems.

After decades of soaring inequality, U.S. society is grotesquely distorted. The richest among us have far more money than they know what to do with, while 27 million Americans are facing a pandemic without health insurance and 22 million newly unemployed people are now navigating a stingy and dysfunctional safety net. It's outrageous that a vast surge of charitable giving is urgently required to keep so many people from going hungry and losing their homes. Our government should be able to do that, just like it should be able to rapidly scale testing, secure vital medical equipment, and speed vaccine development.

If anything good comes out of a horrifying crisis that is hitting the most vulnerable the hardest, it will be a new commitment to building a strong public sector and raising the revenue needed to fund a government that can truly take care of its citizens.

Achieving that goal will mean reducing the bloated concentration of wealth at the top of the income ladder—since it's the rich who can afford to pay higher taxes. Likewise, deep-pocketed U.S. corporations like Amazon and Walmart can easily afford to pay their workers better wages and benefits. No amount of charitable giving by Jeff Bezos or the Walton family can ever be a substitute for making the businesses they control do right for workers and communities.

Still, like it or not, big philanthropy is here to stay. And thanks to five stubborn realities, the giving of billionaires will actually become more important going forward, not less. While public policy can and should work to downsize the upper class and upsize government, reversing the trends of recent decades, we're going to need the rich to give at higher levels going forward than they do now as the public sector inevitably falls short.

Here are the five realities I'm talking about.

### 1. Even with vastly higher taxes on the rich, the U.S. will continue to have a lot of billionaires.

Higher taxes on the rich are a must and would shrink their ranks—and influence—over time. But that would be a very slow process. If Congress embraced the most radical tax plan ever put forth by a presidential candidate—the wealth tax proposed by Senator Bernie Sanders, with a top rate of 8%—and that tax worked effectively (a very big "if," according to many experts), it would slow the creation of huge new fortunes. But the wealth of today's richest Americans wouldn't shrink all that much. The historic average rate of return of the stock market is 10%. And of course, the wealthy can invest in assets that often do a lot better than that. Billionaires aren't going away anytime soon.

### 2. Even if far higher taxes on billionaires did make a significant dent in their fortunes, they'd still have plenty of money for philanthropy.

In 2017, the wealthiest U.S. households gave away just 1.2% of their assets—a paltry slice of their money, but enough to give these donors a huge footprint in society. A far less rich billionaire class that gave away a higher percentage of their wealth—say, 2%—could still wield enormous influence through their giving. The fact is that big philanthropy doesn't actually cost that much, relative to the wealth of billionaires. Some of the most influential members of the donor class, like Tom Steyer, are only worth a few billion dollars. Donors like him, who focus their giving on politics and public policy can get a lot of bang for the buck. Today, even after the market's retreat, there are 383 Americans with assets over $5 billion. Before the crash, some 75,000 U.S. households had investable assets of at least $30 million. Cut those numbers in half, and the donor class would still be here.

## 3. Changing laws won't get rid of big philanthropy.

Various proposals have been floated in recent years aimed at limiting the charitable giving and also reducing the influence of such giving on politics and public policy. None of these reforms are likely to do much. Even if we got rid of the charitable tax break altogether for wealthy givers, they'd still give heavily to advance the causes they care about. Just look at the billions in non-tax-deductible donations that flow into elections. In my book, "The Givers," I laid out ideas for limiting tax-deductible giving to influence public policy. But I'm not optimistic these or similar reform ideas will ever go anywhere, given that nonprofit policy groups across the political spectrum are all dependent on charitable gifts. And even if reforms were enacted, wealth would likely still find ways to sway policy.

## 4. Government will continue to fall short.

The COVID-19 crisis has underscored the need for huge new investments to address glaring inequities and cope with major challenges like climate change and future pandemics. But while a wealth tax and other higher taxes on the rich could go a long way toward helping to pay for these new initiatives, there's still the problem of the massive budgetary shortfalls that loom ahead as the cost of current government programs balloons. Look through the CBO's latest Long-term Budget Outlook, and you'll see what I mean. Even before the pandemic threw the federal government even deeper in the red, the CBO projected that "Large budget deficits over the next 30 years are projected to drive federal debt held by the public to unprecedented levels." Many state and local governments also face huge shortfalls as a result of underfunded pension obligations.

The truth is that just paying for the government we already have—never mind the additional new investments we need—will require not only raising taxes on the wealthy; it will require raising taxes on the upper-middle class, too, and probably the middle class. Progressive critics of billionaires rarely mention these inconvenient fiscal facts. Instead, they peddle the fantasy that if billionaires were properly taxed, government would have all the money it needs. Dream on.

## 5. Philanthropy will become even more important.

Looking ahead, two facts are crystal clear: First, we'll never have enough government to address all our nation's needs, thanks to the long-term fiscal crunch at the federal, state and local levels. And second, we'll continue to have lots of billionaires with plenty of money to spare. The vision of downsizing the billionaire class and upsizing the public sector can drive a lot of positive change. But make no mistake: it can only get us so far.

As a result, like it or not, big philanthropy—and the urgent need for more of it—will remain a major feature of American life going forward. The real question that critics of billionaire giving need to focus on is not "how do we get rid of these plutocrats?" Rather, it is "how can we encourage the super-rich to give much more in ways that meet the pressing needs of the most vulnerable people in America and the world, don't further amplify their already outsized influence, and help to shift who has power in society?"

This kind of big philanthropy is no pipe dream. We can see it in the giving of donors like George Soros, or most recently, the billionaire couple that created the Libra Foundation, Susan and Nicholas Pritzker. I can name other examples, too. What we need is more giving like this. Some changes in charitable laws could help push giving by the wealthy in the right direction. But ultimately, changes in norms and practices will be much more important.

At Inside Philanthropy, we've often explored the question of how to achieve such a sea change in giving. We'll be writing more on this challenging topic in the months ahead, as America emerges from pandemic into what hopefully will be a very different political moment.

Viewpoint 2

> *"While motivations for using fake news may vary, fake news consistently undermines citizens' ability to participate in the governance of their country and make important decisions regarding the fate of their nation."*

# Fake News Endangers Democracy

*Center for Information Technology and Society*

*One of the biggest criticisms of big tech is its unwillingness or inability to prevent the spread of fake news. This viewpoint from the Center for Information Technology and Society looks at a variety of ways false social media content is used to intensify social conflict, undermine trust in the democratic process, and keep citizens distracted from important issues. In numerous ways, fake news has a detrimental effect on democracy. The Center for Information Technology is an organization dedicated to research and education about the cultural and social impacts of technology that is located on the campus of the University of California, Santa Barbara.*

As you read, consider the following questions:

1. How does this viewpoint define "fake news"?

"The Danger of Fake News in Inflaming or Suppressing Social Conflict," Center for Information Technology and Society. Reprinted by permission.

2. What examples does this viewpoint give of false news stories being used to intensify social conflict and influence elections?
3. According to this viewpoint, are efforts by social media companies to police false stories having an effect?

Fake news—news articles that are intentionally and verifiably false designed to manipulate people's perceptions of reality—has been used to influence politics and promote advertising. But it has also become a method to stir up and intensify social conflict. Stories that are untrue and that intentionally mislead readers have caused growing mistrust among American people. In some cases, this mistrust results in incivility, protest over imaginary events, or violence. This unravels the fabric of American life, turning neighbor against neighbor. Why would anyone do this? People, organizations, and governments—foreign governments and even our own—use fake news for two different reasons. First, they intensify social conflict to undermine people's faith in the democratic process and people's ability to work together [1]. Second, they distract people from important issues so that these issues remain unresolved. This section explores how fake news is used for distraction and intensifying conflict.

## Pizzagate

In one infamous case, a fake news story (and the comments people attached to it) moved one man to shoot up a pizzeria that was linked by bogus statements to human trafficking and a presidential candidate. In the incident nicknamed "Pizzagate," a man with a semi-automatic rifle walked into a regular Washington, DC pizza joint—Comet Ping Pong—and fired shots. Why? He was convinced that the pizzeria contained a hidden pedophilia trafficking ring led by Hillary Clinton and her presidential campaign. Where did he come up with this notion? Alt-right communities first created this piece of fiction, and fake news websites promoted the lie by citing specific locations such Comet Ping Pong. It was then tweeted further by people in the Czech Republic, Cyprus, and Vietnam, as well as many bots, getting the story much additional attention. Fake news —political in nature—influenced a man to fire shots inside this restaurant, nearly killing innocent people. The spread of information that was knowingly false had potentially deadly consequences [2].

## Intensifying Social Conflict

People with malicious intent can use fake news to make American national conflicts more intense. Politically motivated fake news came from multiple sources: foreign governments, such as the Russian Internet Research Agency; American political operatives who used illegitimately-acquired Facebook data from the Cambridge Analytica firm to convince social media users how to vote; and from politically motivated groups, such as the alt-right, alt-left, and conspiracy theorists. Despite their different goals, they spread similar fake news stories.

### Russia's Internet Research Agency

During and after the 2016 election, Russian agents created social media accounts to spread fake news that stirred protests and favored presidential candidate Donald Trump while discrediting candidate Hillary Clinton and her associates. They paid Facebook for advertisements that appeared on that site to spread fake news and turn Americans against one another. The U.S. Congressional Intelligence committees responsible for investigating fake news have released 3,500 of these advertisements to the public.

Ads focused on controversial social issues such as race, the Black Lives Matter movement, the 2nd Amendment, immigration, and other issues. The Russians even went so far as to stage protests and counter protests about a given issue, literally having Americans fight one another.

### Cambridge Analytica

Cambridge Analytica was a company that specialized in using data from social media to build psychological profiles about social media users in various countries. It acquired data for 87 million Facebook users without the users' knowledge or consent [3]. With these data—specifically a person's "Likes"—they were able to predict people's political preferences and issue interests. Political campaign operatives coordinated by Donald Trump's chief strategist, Steve Bannon, used this information to target political advertisements and memes on Facebook that mainly focused on discrediting Hillary Clinton's presidential campaign and influencing Americans on a number of pro-Trump issues [4]. These messages were often inflammatory, sensationalistic, sometimes violent, and false. They exploited data that many Americans never agreed to share with advertisers.

### Other Political Groups

Another major effort to disrupt American society has been to fuel fires of suspicion and conspiracy in the wake of major social tragedies—mass shootings, in particular. Conspiracy theorists were fed, and quickly reposted content that originated from Russian agents, political campaign operatives, and other fake news sources, which claimed that these shootings were staged (usually, they claimed, to fool people into supporting gun restrictions). People shared these messages across their social networks. Professor Kate Starbird at the University of Washington assessed this ripple effect by analyzing the links from tweets to websites and comments that promoted the belief that the mass shootings weren't real [5]. Her computer program collected tweets with hashtags that included terms like "false flag," "crisis actor," and "staged." Overall, she collected 99,474 tweets from 15,150 users. The tweets referenced 117 websites, 80 of which were "alternative media," or fake news. Additionally, 44 websites had a clear political agenda: 22 were alt-right, 4 were alt-left, and 7 were anti-globalist.

Fake news poses a serious threat to American democracy. During the 2016 US presidential election, fake news was more prevalent on social media than genuine news and it's unclear whether interventions from Facebook and Twitter and the U.S. government changed this in subsequent elections. Although social media companies are attempting to slow the spread of misinformation by implementing fact-checking programs, these tactics to identify, flag, and remove misinformation, especially regarding the COVID-19 vaccines, are not as effective as they should be. This places additional responsibility on social media users to recognize Fake News and report these posts or avoid interacting with them altogether [6]. Over 62% of Americans receive their news from social media [7]. This makes a large portion of the public vulnerable, because people who read fake news are very likely to believe it. Regardless who posts it, fake news intentionally undermines trust in the news and the government.

### Fake News and the 2020 Black Lives Matter Protests

In the summer of 2020, George Floyd's death sparked outrage in America and led to thousands of Black Lives Matter protests across the country. With BLM a leading topic across mainstream media, the prevalence of fake news on social media led to increased racial and political divides in the U.S. Misinformation, fake news articles, and falsely edited images began circulating online about BLM. Graham Brookie, director of the Atlantic Council's Digital Forensic Research Lab, explained that "The combination of evolving events, sustained attention and, most of all, deep existing divisions make this moment a perfect storm for disinformation" [8].

The fake news surrounding BLM negatively impacted the organization itself and even increased prejudice and racism towards African Americans: A 2022 study examined the effect of the portrayals of the BLM movement in fake news on people's attitudes toward African Americans. People exposed to fake news about BLM reported more negative attitudes toward Black people than those exposed to accurate news sources [9]. This study highlights the impact that fake news can have on peoples' perceptions of Black people in America.

To combat fake news, Black Lives Matter dedicated a tab on their website titled Help Us Fight Disinformation, to report suspicious sites and stories that people see online.

## Fake News and Social Conflict Abroad

Americans aren't the only people with a fake news problem. Although Indian police have made some successful efforts to stem the sharing and influence of fake news, the picture is more tragic in Myanmar, where the government appears to ignore or encourage it:

> Facebook has become a breeding ground for pernicious posts about the Rohingya (minority ethnic group). "In particular, the ones that seem most problematic are government channels that have put a lot of propaganda out there, saying everything from the Rohingya are burning their own villages, to showing bodies of soldiers who may be from other conflicts but saying this is the result of a Rohingya attack." [10]

In another case where a government sends fake news to its own citizens, the effort is to stifle conflict rather than arouse it. Many Chinese citizens believe their government has employed as many as 2 million people to spread propaganda on social media and governmental websites [11]. The people are collectively referred to as the 50c Party because they are rumored to receive 50 cents for fake social media posts they make. Researchers have studied the 50c Party using leaked governmental emails containing 43,000 of their posts. They found that 50c Party employees generated about 448 million posts per year. However, the 50c Party isn't aggressive towards foreign governments or Chinese citizens: Its posts praise the Chinese government or Chinese culture in an attempt to create a positive image among Chinese people toward their own government. These posts can be classified as fake news, because the 50c Party misdirects Chinese citizens and masquerades as everyday social media users when they are actually government employees.

Why would a government invest so much money to create fake news? First, when a person hears a statement from multiple people, they are more likely to believe that statement. By hiring many members of the 50c Party and having them post positive messages about China's political landscape, the Chinese government can convince its citizens to be happy with its performance. Second, when a bunch of posts about one topic are released at once, the topic is likely to become more popular or "go viral." This is why the Chinese government does not have the 50c Party post steadily throughout the year. Instead, they post in bursts so that their posts are more likely to become popular. Third, the Chinese government does not release bursts of 50c Party posts at random. Instead, they wait for times when citizens are most likely to be unhappy or to protest.

## Americans Now Officially Prefer Social Media to Newspapers

For the first time, more Americans report getting their news from social media than from a traditional print newspaper.

Now about 20 percent of Americans said they "often" go to social media for news, while about 16 percent often read a print newspaper, according to a Pew Research Center survey conducted over the first two weeks of August.

Break down the survey's 3,425 responses by age and it becomes clear that this trend is likely to increase over time—social media is the most popular source of news for people under 30 years old, with 36 percent saying they use it often and only two percent reading a physical newspaper.

### Race for the Bottom

In spite of this trend, neither the newspaper nor social media are a particularly popular source of news for Americans. Television still dominates 49 percent of the market, and news websites take another 33 percent.

It's not like everyone who used to read the paper every morning suddenly decided to sign into Twitter instead—Pew's data suggest that newspaper readership has been declining steadily while social media use more or less flatlined in 2017.

## Fake News and the 2022 Ukraine & Russia Conflict

The Russian invasion into Ukraine has been classified as World War Wired as thousands of Russians and Ukrainians utilize social media platforms to document the battles. While most of the social media accounts are real people, there is widespread concern about the amount of misinformation across social networking sites.

NewsGuard's Misinformation Monitor, a fact-checking bulletin, reported an investigation in March 2022: Within 40 minutes of joining the TikTok app, accounts were shown misleading content

But TV's reign may be short-lived: television news viewership seems to directly correlate with age—81 percent of people over the age of 65 regularly watch TV news, as do 65 percent of people between 50 and 64 years old. Meanwhile, just 16 percent of Americans under 30 regularly watch TV news. If today's young people keep their preference for digital platforms over more traditional sources of news and that preference continues in future generations, it's possible that TV news will become much less prominent as older generations die off.

### Look, It's Fine

There's no way around it—social media often serves as a breeding ground for misinformation. But before you complain about those damn "kids these days," rest assured that they'll be just fine.

According to the report, younger generations get their news from a far more diverse array of sources than older generations do. They're not just signing into Twitter or Facebook and turning a blind eye to everything else out there—social media is far more prevalent among young people than it is old people, but other sources like news websites and radio news still inform a large percentage of people under thirty.

**"For News, Americans Now Officially Prefer Social Media to Newspapers," by Dan Robitzski, Futurism, December 12, 2018.**

about the war in Ukraine. These claims were both pro-Russian and pro-Ukrainian, but were all false.

At the time of this writing the war in Ukraine is ongoing. Fake news continues to run rampant across social media platforms, and Russian and Ukrainian citizens are being asked to determine what is real and fake news as major social media platforms fail to take down a vast majority of misinformation [12].

## Some Take-Aways

This section demonstrated how fake news can intensify conflict and suppress conversation about social issues. American conspiracy theorists with varying political motives post on social media intending to intensify ongoing national conflicts. Other governments use fake social media posts to keep citizens happy and distract them from important social issues. While motivations for using fake news may vary, fake news consistently undermines citizens' ability to participate in the governance of their country and make important decisions regarding the fate of their nation.

## References

[1] Office of the Director of National Intelligence, "Assessing Russian Activities and Intentions in Recent US Elections," Jan. 06, 2017. https://www.dni.gov/files/documents/ICA_2017_01.pdf (accessed Aug. 03, 2018).

[2] M. Fisher, J. W. Cox, and P. Hermann, "Pizzagate: From Rumor, to Hashtag, to Gunfire in D.C.," Washington Post, Dec. 06, 2018. https://www.washingtonpost.com/local/pizzagate-from-rumor-to-hashtag-to-gunfire-in-dc/2016/12/06/4c7def50-bbd4-11e6-94ac-3d324840106c_story.html (accessed Aug. 03, 2018).

[3] I. Lapowsky, "Facebook Exposed 87 Million Users to Cambridge Analytica," Wired, Apr. 04, 2018. https://www.wired.com/story/facebook-exposed-87-million-users-to-cambridge-analytica/ (accessed Aug. 03, 2018).

[4] M. Rosenberg, N. Confessore, and C. Cadwalladr, "How Trump Consultants Exploited the Facebook Data of Millions," The New York Times, Apr. 02, 2018. https://www.nytimes.com/2018/03/17/us/politics/cambridge-analytica-trump-campaign.html (accessed Aug. 03, 2018).

[5] K. Starbird, "Examining the Alternative Media Ecosystem through the Production of Alternative Narratives of Mass Shooting Events on Twitter," Proceedings of the International AAAI Conference on Web and Social Media (ICWSM 2017), Montreal, Canada, May 2017, pp. 230-239. https://ojs.aaai.org/index.php/ICWSM/article/view/14878

[6] Center for Countering Digital Hate, "The Disinformation Dozen," Center for Countering Digital Hate | CCDH, Mar. 21, 2021. https://counterhate.com/research/the-disinformation-dozen/ (accessed Jun. 27, 2022).
[7] E. Grieco, "More Americans are Turning to Multiple Social Media Sites for News," Pew Research Center, Nov. 02, 2017. http://www.pewresearch.org/fact-tank/2017/11/02/more-americans-are-turning-to-multiple-social-media-sites-for-news/ (accessed Aug. 03, 2018).
[8] C. Georgacopoulos and T. Poche, "Fake News, Disinformation, and the George Floyd Protests," Fight Fake News. https://faculty.lsu.edu/fakenews/about/protestfakenews.php (accessed Jun. 27, 2022).
[9] C. Wright, K. Gatlin, D. Acosta, and C. Taylor, "Portrayals of the Black Lives Matter Movement in Hard and Fake News and Consumer Attitudes Toward African Americans," Howard Journal of Communications, pp. 1–23, Apr. 2022, Accessed: Jun. 28, 2022. [Online]. Available: https://doi.org/10.1080/10646175.2022.2065458
[10] The World Staff, "In Myanmar, Fake News Spread on Facebook Stokes Ethnic Violence," The World from PRX, Nov. 01, 2017. https://theworld.org/stories/2017-11-01/myanmar-fake-news-spread-facebook-stokes-ethnic-violence (accessed Jun. 28, 2022).
[11] G. King, J. Pan, and M. E. Roberts, "How the Chinese Government Fabricates Social Media Posts for Strategic Distraction, not Engaged Argument," American Political Science Review, vol. 111, no. 3, pp. 484–501, 2017. https://doi.org/10.1017/S0003055417000144
[12] S. Brown, "In Russia-Ukraine War, Social Media Stokes Ingenuity, Disinformation," MIT Sloan, Apr. 06, 2022. https://mitsloan.mit.edu/ideas-made-to-matter/russia-ukraine-war-social-media-stokes-ingenuity-disinformation (accessed Jun. 28, 2022).

Viewpoint 3

> *"Americans need to better learn—and schools need to teach—media literacy."*

# Americans Who Get News Mainly on Social Media Are Less Knowledgeable and Less Engaged

*Tom Infield*

*In this viewpoint, Tom Infield examines a report by the Pew Research Center's American News Pathways project that found that Americans who get their news mostly from social media are more likely not only to encounter misinformation, but also to believe it. They are also less knowledgeable in general about political and social issues of importance. By learning media literacy and understanding the distinction between how reputable news organizations and social media operate, people will be able to better identify online misinformation. Tom Infield is a Philadelphia-based journalist and frequent contributor to publications of the Pew Charitable Trust.*

As you read, consider the following questions:

1. How is the American News Pathways project different from other surveys by the Pew Research Center?

"Americans Who Get News Mainly on Social Media Are Less Knowledgeable and Less Engaged," by Tom Infield, The Pew Charitable Trusts, November 16, 2020. Reprinted by permission.

2. What other group was equally as disengaged as the group that gets their news primarily from social media, according to the research discussed in this viewpoint?
3. What is "media literacy" according to this viewpoint, and how could it help with this problem?

How we get our political news can make a big difference in how well-informed we are and in how likely we are to encounter—and believe—misinformation.

A Pew Research Center report published in July shows that Americans who rely primarily on social media for news—which describes about 18% of adults in the U.S.—tend to know less about the 2020 election, less about the coronavirus pandemic, and less about political news in general than people who rely on news websites, cable or network TV, radio, and print.

Those who depend on social media are also more likely than other news consumers to be exposed to made-up news, such as the conspiracy theory that powerful people planned the pandemic and invented the coronavirus in a lab, and to give credence to falsehoods.

These conclusions come from the Center's American News Pathways project, which since last November has been exploring the connection between Americans' news habits and their news awareness. Rather than conducting just a single poll, the news project is taking six deep dives into a pool of nearly 10,000 adults representing a demographic and geographic cross section of the nation who have agreed to periodically be surveyed.

"What the project has done is weave together where people are turning for their news—what their information and news sources are—and how that connects to their perceptions and knowledge about certain events," says Amy Mitchell, the Center's director of journalism research. "It's answering the question: How do people's sense of what's happening in the U.S.—in the world—connect to their information sources?

"The overarching finding," she says, "is that U.S. adults who mainly get their political news through social media tend to be less engaged with news. They follow the news less closely, and they tend to be less knowledgeable on a wide range of current events and broad political-knowledge questions about the U.S."

Over nine months and multiple surveys, Center researchers asked respondents 29 different fact-based questions that touched on a variety of topics related to the news, from economics to President Donald Trump's impeachment and the COVID-19 pandemic. Across the 29 questions, the average proportion that got each question right was lower among Americans who rely most on social media for political news than among those who rely most on other types of news sources (except for local TV).

The percentage of American adults who use social media for news, sometimes or often, is now at 55%, Mitchell says—up from the presidential election of 2016, when 42% of adults got at least some news from social media.

The report also found that just 8% of Americans who prefer social media for news are closely following this year's election, compared with four times as many who get news mainly from cable TV (37%) or print (33%). Only adults who depend on local TV stations for their news are comparable to the social media group in their low attention to the election.

Nearly three-quarters of adults (71%) are active on Facebook, and about half (52%) draw at least some news from there, Mitchell says. The next most important source is YouTube. Other sources include Twitter, Instagram, LinkedIn, Snapchat, and WhatsApp.

Overall, social media ranks second among all forms of media as a pathway to news, the report says. The 18% who mainly get their news this way compares with 25% who rely on news websites, such as those managed by newspapers, news broadcasters, cable networks, and Internet-only providers.

Cable TV and local TV each are the main pathway for 16% of adults. Network TV comes in next at 13%, followed by radio at

8%. The print version of newspapers (as distinguished from their websites) runs last at 3%.

At the same time that social media usage has increased as a news platform, the credibility of traditional news sources has eroded, Mitchell says. Center research conducted last year showed that trust in *The New York Times* and *The Washington Post*, to cite two examples, fell significantly from 2014 to 2019, particularly among Republicans.

And demographic factors play a role in who goes where for news, the report says.

Nearly half of the Americans who focus on social media—48%—are under 30 years old, making them Millennials or members of Generation Z. They are, by far, the youngest group.

At the other end of the age spectrum, older Americans are much more likely to turn first to print or cable or network TV. Of adults who say that print is their most common way of getting news, 47% are 65 or older.

Partly because they're young, people who rely primarily on social media for news have lower incomes and are less likely to hold a college degree than people in the other groups, with the exception of the local TV viewers.

"What strikes me is that the people who get most of their political news from local TV are similar in many respects to people who are getting their news from social media," says Eugene Kiely, director of FactCheck.org, a project of the Annenberg Public Policy Center at the University of Pennsylvania that monitors the factual accuracy of national political figures and acts as a self-described "consumer advocate" for voters.

He says that he wonders if many of the social media users would be sitting on the couch watching local TV news were it not for the advent of Facebook. "There are very interesting parallels," he says.

Kiely calls it "very concerning" that the growing cohort of social media users is paying so little attention to the Nov. 3 election, which he says makes them particularly vulnerable to the sort of deliberate misinformation that came in waves in the late stage of the 2016 presidential race.

As of June, more than a quarter of people who rely most on social media had heard "a lot" about the false story that COVID-19 was deliberately or accidentally created in a lab, and 8 in 10 had heard "a little," the report says. Overall, their awareness of this bogus idea was higher than for any other group.

One-third of these people—36%—said they believed the virus came from a lab, and 27% said they weren't sure. Thirty-five percent said the virus came about naturally.

The most comparable group for believing the misinformation about the virus's origins was, again, the group that gets most of its news from local TV. Within this group, 32% said the virus originated, by mistake or on purpose, in a lab.

Users mainly of social media also had heard more than any others about two unproven theories: that vitamin C can be a protection against the virus and that the latest 5G mobile phone technology somehow is linked to the virus.

While the Americans who rely on social media as their primary news source were the most likely to both hear and believe fake news, they were the least likely (except for the local TV group) to worry that misinformation could impact the election, with only 37% saying they were very concerned about such an eventuality.

Kiely says that while the trend toward social media as a major news pathway is sure to accelerate, it's a development that is neither good nor bad on its own. But, he adds, Americans need to better learn—and schools need to teach—media literacy.

"People should understand how news operates—what reputable news organizations do in terms of disclosing their funding, disclosing their financial ties, disclosing their staff biographies," Kiely says. "So much of the misinformation that floats on social media is not attributed to anybody."

Viewpoint 4

> *"This is not a case of Big Tech violating the president or other users' First Amendment rights, but better understood as their decision to exercise their own."*

# Banning Users Is Not a Violation of the First Amendment by Big Tech

*Jennifer Huddleston*

*Tech companies such as Facebook, Twitter, and Amazon have been criticized for violating the rights of individuals they've banned from their sites. In this viewpoint, Jennifer Huddleston argues that because these companies are not state actors, they cannot violate the rights of individuals by refusing to do business with them. As long as the government doesn't tell private tech companies which users to ban, there are no state actors involved in the decision, and it is the right of private companies to choose with whom they do business. Jennifer Huddleston is the former director of technology and innovation policy for the American Action Forum, and is now policy counsel for NetChoice.*

As you read, consider the following questions:

1. According to Huddleston, why is it important that technology companies are not state actors or the public square?

"No, Big Tech Did Not Violate the First Amendment," by Jennifer Huddleston, American Action Forum, January 12, 2021.

2. What are common criticisms—from the Left and the Right—of Section 230?
3. What examples of hypocrisy does Huddleston mention?

Following the riot at the United States Capitol, many prominent tech companies have taken steps to deplatform or remove various individuals and services that have been associated with the violence. Twitter, Facebook, and Instagram have all suspended President Donald Trump's accounts. Apple and Google removed alternative social media app Parler from their app stores for hosting content associated with the violence at the Capitol and a continued failure to engage in moderation to prevent further incitement to violence. Other smaller platforms have also taken steps to limit the use of their services. For example, payment processor Stripe and shopping service Shopify suspended their services from several Trump campaign-associated sources. Some have criticized these moves as unfair discrimination and argued that they represent censorship or violate the First Amendment. Others have raised concerns that these moves reflect an overconcentration of power in the hands of the largest tech companies in a way that stifles speech and harms the free flow of ideas. These critics have made renewed calls for tech regulation and potential modification to Section 230, a liability shield that protects content moderation decisions, and allegations that "Big Tech" companies are monopolies.

## Private Actors and the First Amendment

Twitter, Facebook, Amazon, and other private companies have decided to remove accounts or suspend services. It is often forgotten, however, that these companies have First Amendment rights themselves. They are allowed to decide what content to carry via their terms of service and whom to allow to have accounts.

No state actors silenced voices nor compelled these companies to remove the content. As a result, there is not a First Amendment violation. The courts have repeatedly held that private social media is neither a "public square" nor a state actor that must uphold the First Amendment. As such, any cases involving these bans are likely to fail.

In the past, many on the right have defended the rights of private companies to make decisions about whom to associate with or what cakes to bake. These rights have their limits when it comes to civil rights laws concerning discrimination, but in general companies are allowed to decide whom to do business with. Social media platforms and other online services are providing conduits for speech that have been a great advantage to a wide range of individuals and viewpoints that might have been ignored or too small for traditional media, including conservative voices.

Even more than the typical user, the president is far from without a microphone. More easily than any other American or policymaker, he could directly address the American public through traditional media means. This is not a case of Big Tech violating the president or other users' First Amendment rights, but better understood as their decision to exercise their own.

## The Impact of Section 230

Section 230—the law that provides liability protection for online platforms from suits over user-generated content, allowing them to engage in content moderation as they see fit—has also faced further criticism in light of the recent decisions by platforms and the use of social media platforms by bad actors. For example, following Twitter's decision to ban President Trump, Senator Lindsey Graham (R-SC) tweeted, "I'm more determined than ever to strip Section 230 protections from Big Tech (Twitter) that let them be immune from lawsuits." But removing Section 230 would be unlikely to have changed the actions that occurred and in fact would likely lead many platforms to moderate content even more aggressively.

Because of Section 230, online platforms can allow controversial ideas to be discussed on their services (within the limits of federal law) and not fear that they will be sued for carrying such content.

There are notable limitations to this liability protection, such as child pornography and sex trafficking, but in most cases platforms are free to make their own decisions regarding what content is allowed on their service. They are also allowed to determine how they enforce these guidelines, what content violates them, and what if any users to remove.

Without Section 230, platforms could be held liable for controversial content posted by their users. Thus, platforms would face a moderator's dilemma of either engaging in heavy-handed moderation to prevent anything potentially offensive or harmful (that could trigger a suit against the platform for hosting it) or not engaging in moderation at all. Most online platforms would probably choose to engage in the heavy-handed moderation, since as Reddit co-founder Alexis Ohanian pointed out in a Tweet, "What they all eventually learn is users WANT moderation."

Those on the right do not hold a monopoly on the criticisms of Section 230; many on the left have criticized it for some time. Considering the role of apps such as Parler in the violence and the criticism by some on the left that mainstream platforms did not take action against President Trump's accounts soon enough, the criticism of Section 230 is likely to continue from both sides of the aisle. It is important to remember, however, that overzealous content moderation would not apply to only one viewpoint or to the material one side does not like. The risk of potentially company-crushing litigation could chill companies from carrying speech around any number of controversial topics, such as the #MeToo movement, for fear that they could be liable for defamation or other harms. The result would be that important conversations about controversial topics would be more limited and more difficult to have.

There will be many concerns about the role of social media in the events of January 6 and many concerns about the decisions made regarding accounts and services in the aftermath. Changes to Section 230, however, would likely stifle non-harmful speech around sensitive topics as well .

## Big Tech's Actions Are Not Evidence of a Lack of Competition

Finally, some of the president's supporters and conservative technology critics have pointed to the recent actions—particularly by Apple, Google, and Amazon against the alternative social media site Parler that have led to the service being offline—as evidence that Big Tech is too powerful. These companies hold a monopolistic position that stifles not only competition but speech, the argument goes, and requires an antitrust response. But the internet is far more than Big Tech, and these actions themselves do not necessarily indicate collusion.

Some are alleging that the large tech companies are coordinating their actions to silence conservative voices. For its part, Parler has filed an antitrust lawsuit against AWS for its decision to stop hosting its product, alleging collusion between the website-hosting service and Twitter, Parler's primary competition. These allegations of a conspiracy are unlikely to succeed, as there is no plausibility based on the complaint that such an agreement exists. Many online platforms have similar guidelines that govern the use of their app stores or services, and so it makes sense that they would react in a similar way to a broad phenomenon. For example, Apple removed Parler for hosting objectionable content in the form of calls of direct threats for violence and failing to develop sufficient levels of moderation guidelines to respond to this objectionable content. Amazon Web Services (AWS) informed Parler it would cease to provide services for failing to remove content that is an incitement to violence, and such a decision could easily be grounded in the company's own acceptable use policy. It seems unlikely that collusion is driving these decisions rather than broader social pressures.

Some of the complaints about these decisions smack of hypocrisy. Just recently, some advocates for regulating Big Tech, including Senator Josh Hawley, applauded MasterCard for terminating the use of its services on Pornhub and urged other payment services to do the same. Now that a similar action has been taken against Parler, however, some of these same critics are alleging that "tech giants" are conspiring against conservatives rather than exercising their rights as private companies and enforcing their own policies.

Looking more broadly, Amazon and app stores were never the only options for server-hosting and access to consumers. While Amazon may be a leader in cloud services, there are numerous other competitors including Oracle and IBM from which Parler could attempt to negotiate services. Parler's creators also could have chosen to make the app available for direct download rather than through an app store. In short, Parler is reaping the consequences of the choices its founders made, not facing a conspiracy of Big Tech to remove a competitor.

To be sure, some have raised questions about whether policymakers should distinguish between decisions made at the level of individual sites and decisions made at a more foundational level (for example, website hosts or internet service providers). Such an approach would most likely require such services to be treated as a utility and result in significant changes to Internet business models and consumers. Such an approach would be a significant policy change and the complete impact of such a shift cannot be addressed in full here. These companies are private actors with their own terms of service who are allowed to make their decisions about whom to provide services to within the bounds of their terms of service and current law. Policymakers and consumers should be concerned about calls to use antitrust enforcement against Big Tech in regard to private companies' choices to enforce their policies. Private antitrust litigation can result in higher prices or fewer options for consumers. Legislative action could have an even greater impact, as it could include content moderation decisions as a potential actionable harm for antitrust. Proposals to break up Big Tech would not resolve concerns about content moderation or access to services. After all, smaller companies would still face decisions about whom to allow to use their services and in the case of harmful or unpopular content have the same incentives to choose whom to serve.

The technology ecosystem remains an innovative and dynamic market. Choosing to change antitrust laws to achieve preferred outcomes regarding Big Tech would not only likely fail to achieve those outcomes, but also harm consumers and a vibrant sector of the economy.

## Conclusion

Whether you applaud or detest the recent decisions made by online platforms, it is important to remember that these are private actors and not the government. While these actions did not violate the First Amendment, many policy proposals in response could yield greater intervention by the government into speech and private actions that would give rise to First Amendment concerns. The internet is far more than just Big Tech.

## Periodical and Internet Sources Bibliography

*The following articles have been selected to supplement the diverse views presented in this chapter.*

Susie Alegre, "We're Dangerously Close to Giving Big Tech Control of Our Thoughts," *Time*, June 29, 2022. https://time.com/6191973/big-tech-freedom-of-thought/.

Praharsha Anand, "The Pros and Cons of Breaking Up Big Tech," ITPro, February 17, 2022. https://www.itpro.com/data-insights/big-data/358795/pros-and-cons-of-breaking-up-big-tech.

Carmen Ang, "How Do Big Tech Giants Make Their Billions?" Visual Capitalist, April 25, 2022. https://www.visualcapitalist.com/how-big-tech-makes-their-billions-2022/.

Bill Baer and Caitlin Chin, "Addressing Big Tech's Power over Speech," Brookings Institution, June 1, 2021. https://www.brookings.edu/blog/techtank/2021/06/01/addressing-big-techs-power-over-speech/.

Alison Beard, "Can Big Tech Be Disrupted?" *Harvard Business Review*, January–February 2022. https://hbr.org/2022/01/can-big-tech-be-disrupted.

Rodrigo Fernandez, Ilke Adriaans, Tobias J. Klinge, and Reijer Hendrikse, "How Big Tech Is Becoming the Government," SOMO, February 5, 2021. https://www.somo.nl/how-big-tech-is-becoming-the-government/.

Brian Fishman, "What It Really Means to Hold Big Tech Accountable," Lawfare, September 16, 2022. https://www.lawfareblog.com/what-it-really-means-hold-big-tech-accountable.

Thomas Lambert, "What's Behind the War on Big Tech?" Cato Institute, Fall 2021. https://www.cato.org/regulation/fall-2021/whats-behind-war-big-tech.

Stephen Maher, "Transparency Is Key to Curbing the Power of Big Tech," Centre for International Governance Innovation, August 2, 2021. https://www.cigionline.org/articles/transparency-is-key-to-curbing-the-power-of-big-tech/.

John Naughton, "Can Big Tech Ever Be Reined In?" *Guardian*, November 21, 2021. https://www.theguardian.com/technology/2021/nov/21/can-big-tech-ever-be-reined-in.

Shira Ovide, "Why Is Big Tech Under Assault? Power," *New York Times*, April 21, 2021. https://www.nytimes.com/2021/04/21/technology/big-tech-power.html.

# For Further Discussion

## Chapter 1

1. The viewpoint by Marc Goedhart and Tim Koller argues that a short-term outlook is to blame for the fact that big corporations are out of step with the public interest. Do you agree? How does the profit structure of corporations contribute to this problem?
2. In the viewpoint by Matt Gitsham, Ajit Nayak, and Jonathan Gosling, the authors argue that corporate leaders can play an important role in influencing the government to take more action against climate change. However, the viewpoint by Christopher Wright and Daniel Nyberg argues that corporate leadership on environmental action tends to dissolve quickly. Which argument do you find more convincing? What are some ways corporations could be convinced to continue supporting climate action?
3. The viewpoint by Nishant Bagadia mentions the socially responsible outdoor clothing company Patagonia. Since that viewpoint was written, the owner of Patagonia has donated the company to a trust that will use the company's profits to combat climate change and protect the world's remaining undeveloped land. Do you think other companies will follow suit? Why or why not?

## Chapter 2

1. Public television and public radio (PBS and NPR) were intended to be a source of news and information for everyone, but according to the viewpoint by Christopher Chávez, the economic realities have forced them to cater to people who can afford to donate money to support the programming. This is different from the way Britain's public media is funded, as discussed in the viewpoint by Joshua

Benton. Do you think a similar funding plan would work in the U.S.? Why or why not?

2. According to the viewpoint by Sarah Repucci, human rights go hand in hand with economic interests. Do you agree with her argument? Why or why not?
3. According to research cited in viewpoints by Joshua Benton and Alina Ladyzhensky, the United States is now considered a "flawed democracy." What do you think that means, and why might the U.S. fall into that category? Do you agree with that assessment? If so, what do you think can be done to improve the health of democracy in the United States?

## Chapter 3

1. In Sergio Sismondo's viewpoint on corruption in medical research, the author quotes the philosopher Søren Kierkegaard, who wrote, "As the world changes, the forms of corruption also gradually become more cunning, more difficult to point out." Can you think of examples, other than in medical research, of how corporate corruption of our world has become so ingrained that it is difficult to see?
2. In the viewpoint about the public's perception of industry-supported science by John C. Besley, Aaron M. McCright, Joseph D. Martin, Kevin Elliot, and Nagwan Zahry, the authors point out that in the first few decades after World War II, the public tended to *prefer* industry-supported science. Why do you think that has changed?
3. Several authors in this chapter point out that despite the large amount of money the country spends on health care, the U.S. ranks below most other advanced nations in terms of health outcomes for its people. This is despite the U.S. having some of the most high-tech health care in the world. How might this discrepancy be explained?

## Chapter 4

1. Jennifer Huddleston argues that it is not a violation of users' First Amendment rights when tech companies like Twitter choose to ban users. Do you find her argument convincing? Why or why not? What obligation should tech companies have to protect their users' rights to free speech?
2. In his viewpoint, David Callahan argues that in order to pay for all the government needs to do, we would need to raise taxes not just on the wealthy but the middle class as well. Politically that's a hard sell. Do you think Americans pay enough taxes? Why are people unwilling to pay more taxes if it results in more government services, such as health care and education?
3. The viewpoint by Tom Infield includes coverage of a report finding that people who get most of their news from social media are less knowledgeable about issues and more likely to believe falsehoods they encounter. What sources of news do you think would be better? How would one go about finding and vetting news sources if one wanted to be a well-informed citizen?

# Organizations to Contact

*The editors have compiled the following list of organizations concerned with the issues debated in this book. The descriptions are derived from materials provided by the organizations. All have publications or information available for interested readers. The list was compiled on the date of publication of the present volume; the information provided here may change. Be aware that many organizations take several weeks or longer to respond to inquiries, so allow as much time as possible.*

**Alliance for Research on Corporate Sustainability (ARCS)**

Ross School of Business
701 Tappan Avenue
Ann Arbor, MI 48109
email: arcs.information@gmail.com
website: https://corporate-sustainability.org

The ARCS is a partnership of academic institutions that create and share data that can aid in developing and pursuing research on corporate responsibility. The alliance focuses on academic research on policies and strategies for creating sustainable businesses.

**Boston College Center for Corporate Citizenship (BCCCC)**

Carroll School of Management
140 Commonwealth Avenue
Chestnut Hill, MA 02467
(617) 552-4545
website: https://ccc.bc.edu

The Boston College Center for Corporate Citizenship is an organization dedicated to helping businesses become better corporate citizens. The organization provides research, executive education, tools, and networking opportunities for its hundreds of corporate members on sustainable and socially conscious corporate development.

**Center for Democracy and Technology (CDT)**

1401 K Street NW, Suite 200
Washington, DC 20005
(202) 637-9800
website: https://cdt.org

The CDT works to influence technology policy and the architecture of the internet that impacts citizens' daily lives in order to strengthen individual freedoms and rights. It does this by championing laws and policies that protect against invasive technology-related practices and empower people to use technology for good and insisting on transparency from online platforms.

**Corporate Accountability**

10 Milk Street, Suite 610
Boston, MA 02108
(617) 695-2525
email: Info@CorporateAccountability.org
website: www.corporateaccountability.org

This organization works to stop transnational organizations from devastating democracy, the environment, and human rights. It also aims to create a world where corporations answer to people, not the other way around.

**Generation Citizen**

PO Box 200441
South Ozone Park, NY 11420
website: https://generationcitizen.org

Generation Citizen is an organization dedicated to empowering young people to become engaged and effective citizens by providing them with the knowledge and skills to participate in democracy. It accomplishes this by inspiring civic participation through a state standards-aligned action civics class.

**Green America**

1612 K Street NW, Suite 1000
Washington, DC 20006
(800) 584-7336
website: www.greenamerica.org

Green America uses the economic power of consumers, investors, businesses, and the marketplace to help create a more socially just and environmentally sustainable society. It works to accomplish this by educating consumers, empowering small businesses to go green, and incorporate social and environmental solutions into the supply chain.

**Law and Economics Center of George Mason University, Antonin Scalia Law School (LEC)**

3301 Fairfax Drive
Hazel Hall, Suite 440
Arlington, VA 22201
(703) 993-8040
email: LEC@gmu.edu
website: https://masonlec.org

The LEC is a leading academic center for the study and research of economics and law. Many of their articles and educational pieces are accessible for non-experts.

**Move to Amend**

PO Box 188617
Sacramento, CA 95818
(916) 318-8040
website: www.movetoamend.org

With its slogan, "End corporate rule. Legalize democracy," Move to Amend states its aim of amending the U.S. Constitution to clearly state that money is not speech, and to restore the rights of citizens. It is a nonpartisan coalition of individuals and organizations working to end corporate personhood.

**National Endowment for Democracy (NED)**

1025 F Street NW, Suite 800
Washington, DC 20004
(202) 378-9700
email: info@NED.org
website. www.ned.org

The National Endowment for Democracy is a private, nonprofit organization that is dedicated to the growth and strengthening of democratic institutions around the world. It works to foster democratic institutions abroad by supporting political parties, trade unions, free markets, independent media, and the rule of law.

**Union of Concerned Scientists**

2 Brattle Square
Cambridge, MA 02137
(617) 547-5552
website: www.ucsusa.org

The Union of Concerned Scientists is an organization founded in 1969 to encourage science to move away from military technologies and toward research that addresses social and environmental problems. The organization is still dedicated to sharing information, seeking truth, and letting scientific findings guide conclusions.

# Bibliography of Books

Albert Bourla. *Moonshot: Inside Pfizer's Nine-Month Race to Make the Impossible Possible*. New York, NY: Harper Business, 2022.

David Callahan. *The Givers: Wealth, Power, and Philanthropy in a New Gilded Age*. New York, NY: Vintage, 2017.

David Dayen. *Monopolized: Life in the Age of Corporate Power*. New York, NY: The New Press, 2020.

Eamon Doyle, ed. *Is America a Democracy or an Oligarchy?* (At Issue). New York, NY: Greenhaven Publishing, 2021.

Lucie Greene. *Silicon States: The Power and Politics of Big Tech and What It Means for Our Future*. Berkeley, CA: Counterpoint, 2018.

Lisa Idzikowski, ed. *Big Tech and Democracy* (Current Controversies). New York, NY: Greenhaven Publishing, 2022.

Jon Jureidini and Leemon B. McHenry. *The Illusion of Evidence-Based Medicine: Exposing the Crisis of Credibility in Clinical Research*. Adelaide, AU: Wakefield Press, 2020.

Stephanie Kelton. *The Deficit Myth: Modern Monetary Theory and the Birth of the People's Economy*. New York, NY: Public Affairs, 2020.

Christopher Leonard. *Kochland: The Secret History of Koch Industries and Corporate Power in America*. New York, NY: Simon and Schuster, 2019.

Peter Loftus. *The Messenger: Moderna, the Vaccine, and the Business Gamble that Changed the World*. Boston, MA: Harvard Business Review Press, 2022.

Rob Reich, Mehran Sahami, and Jeremy M. Weinstein. *System Error: Where Big Tech Went Wrong and How We Can Reboot*. New York, NY: Harper, 2021.

Klaus Schwab. *Stakeholder Capitalism: A Global Economy that Works for Progress, People, and the Planet*. Hoboken, NJ: John Wiley and Sons, 2021.

George Serafeim. *Purpose and Profit: How Business Can Lift Up the World*. New York, NY: HarperCollins Leadership, 2022.

Matt Stoller. *Goliath: the 100-Year War Between Monopoly Power and Democracy*. New York, NY: Simon and Schuster, 2019.

Zephyr Teachout. *Break 'Em Up: Recovering Our Freedom from Big Ag, Big Tech, and Big Money*. New York, NY: All Points Books, 2020.

Jonathan Tepper. *The Myth of Capitalism: Monopolies and the Death of Competition*. Hoboken, NJ: John Wiley and Sons, 2019.

Tim Wu. *The Curse of Bigness: Antitrust in the New Gilded Age*. New York, NY: Columbia Global Reports, 2018.

# Index


## A

age, 146–147, 153
Amazon, 15, 30, 40–42, 48, 132, 135, 155–156, 159–160
American News Pathways, 150–151
American Trends Panel (ATP), 74–76
Apple, 15, 132, 156, 159
Australia, 80, 83

## B

banks, 22, 31, 37
  World Bank, 31, 63–65
B corporations (B corps), 38–41
Berkshire Hathaway, 40
bias, 57, 103
billionaires, 16, 48, 131–132, 134–136, 138
  Bezos, Jeff, 48, 135
  Branson, Richard, 36
  Zuckerberg, Mark, 14
biomedical meta-analyses, 94
B Lab, 40
Black Lives Matter (BLM), 142, 144
BlackRock, 40, 42, 44
brand, 23, 43, 57, 84
Britain, 77–78, 118, 164
  British Broadcasting Corporation (BBC), 51, 77–78, 82
Business Roundtable, 21, 23, 26

## C

capitalism, 14–15, 20, 22, 40–42, 44, 48
CEOs, 28–30, 32, 40
China, 23, 62–64, 145
climate change, 14–15, 18, 20–21, 26, 28–31, 34–39, 137, 164
clinical trials, 98, 102–104, 114
competition, 36, 94, 123–125, 128, 159
consolidation, 15, 123–125
consumers, 24–25, 27, 42–44, 52, 123–124, 126, 151, 153, 160–161
contract research organizations (CROs), 99, 104
corporate social responsibility (CSR), 42
Corporation for Public Broadcasting (CPB), 48–53
  National Public Radio (NPR), 48, 50–53, 75, 78, 95, 164
  Public Broadcasting Station (PBS), 48, 51–53, 77–79, 164
  Tovares, Joseph, 52
corruption, 64–65, 88, 99–101, 103–108, 165
COVID-19 (coronavirus pandemic), 101, 133–134, 137, 144, 151–154
Cuba, 63, 119

## D

debt, 64, 72, 75
  federal, 137

democracy, 15, 48, 55–56, 62, 66, 77, 79–80, 83–84, 86–88, 90, 132, 140, 143, 165
*Economist's, The,* Democracy Index, 88–89
"Funding Democracy: Public Media and Democratic Health in 33 Countries," 79, 87
diversity, 50, 52–53, 118
doctors (physicians), 104, 106, 116–122, 124, 127
*Dodge v. Ford Motor Co.,* 41
drug industry, 94–95, 97

# E

economy, 22, 24–25, 36, 64, 87, 161
global, 66
*Political Economy of Media, The,* 51
elections, 58, 60, 64, 88, 137, 141, 143, 153
employees (workers), 21–25, 27, 36, 41–42, 65–66, 97, 105, 119, 135, 145,
environment, 11, 18, 21, 23, 27, 30, 36–37, 40, 63–64, 114
environmental, social, and governance (ESG), 22
externalities, 25–26

# F

"fake news," 101, 140–145, 147–148, 154
farmers, 31
Floyd, George, 144
Ford Motor Company, 41
fossil fuels, 29, 31, 38
Freedom House, 62–66

# G

Gap, 42
GDP, 80–81, 88–89
gender, 23, 43
"ghost-management," 105–107
Gilberg, Jay Coen, 40–41
globalization, 20, 24
Google, 15, 22, 30, 132, 156, 159
government, 11, 14–15, 25–26, 28–32, 35, 48, 54, 56, 58–60, 64, 68, 70–72, 74–75, 80, 87-89, 112–113, 115–119, 132–138, 143–146, 155, 161, 164, 166
grafting, 100, 107
Great Depression, 20
Greece, 64
"green bonds," 31
Guayaki Brands, 42

# H

health care, 11, 40–41, 78, 94, 116–117, 123–124, 126–128, 165–166
Affordable Care Act (ACA), 53, 124, 126
Beveridge Model, 118–119
Bismarck Model, 119
National Health Insurance Model (NHI), 117–119
out-of-pocket model, 119
hospitals, 104, 116–117, 120–122, 125
human rights, 28, 63, 66, 88, 165

# I

immigrants, 84

income, 20–21, 42, 51, 67, 69, 70–71, 73, 121, 135
India, 55–57, 59, 61, 65, 83
industry-funded research, 105, 114
insurance, 14, 35, 37, 117–119, 121, 135
Iran, 63–64

## J

J.P. Morgan, 40
Jefferson, Thomas, 14

## L

laws (legislation), 56, 60
  antitrust, 20, 124, 126, 159–161
Lego, 23
LGBTQ community, 53
lobbying, 28–29, 31–32
Lou, Ratto, 30

## M

manufacturing, 24, 35, 38, 56
media literacy, 132, 150–151, 154
medicine, 15, 103
millennials, 43, 153
misinformation, 18, 144, 147–148, 150–151, 154
Mulvaney, Mick, 50
Myanmar, 64, 145

## N

National Academies of Science, Engineering, and Medicine, 112
Neff, Timothy, 79–80, 82–83, 86–88
Nestlé, 29

## O

Obama, Barack, 30, 44

## P

Patagonia, 43
patients, 94–95, 116, 118, 120, 124
pension, 26, 137
pharmaceutical companies, 95, 99–102, 104, 106–107, 114
philanthropy, 132–139
Pickard, Victor, 79–80, 82–83, 86–88
poverty, 11, 14, 22
profit, 18–19, 34–35, 38, 40–42, 58, 68–69, 75, 84, 94, 114, 117–121, 164
Public Broadcasting Act of 1967, 50
public sphere, 53

## R

regulation, 15, 20, 30, 32, 36, 38, 80, 94, 119, 123–127, 156
renewable energy, 28–29, 31–32, 36
Russia, 142, 147

## S

Section 230, 156–158
shareholders, 18–24, 26–27, 35, 37, 41, 94
short-termism, 21–22, 25
social media, 132, 140, 142–145, 147–148, 150–154, 156–159, 166

Facebook (Meta), 14–15, 132, 142–143, 145, 152–153, 155–156
Parler, 158–160
Twitter, 143, 146–147, 152, 156–157, 159, 166
sponsorship, 98, 104–105, 107
subsidies, 31–32, 83
surveys, 74–75, 150–152
sustainability, 26, 31–32, 36–37, 43
eco-efficiency practices, 36

## T

taxes, 26, 66, 82, 118, 133–138, 166
technology, 20, 56, 70, 80, 117, 132, 140, 154–155, 159, 161
television (TV), 51, 53, 56–61, 77–78, 164, 151-154
"trickle-up economics," 40, 43
Trump, Donald, 43, 50, 142–143, 152, 156–158
trust, 15, 41, 80, 95, 99–101, 114, 121, 141
democracy, 140, 144
doctor-patient relationship, 120
media, 153
scientific research, 15, 111–114

## U

Ukraine, 147–148
United Nations (UN), 29, 101
United States Capitol riot, 156

## V

values, 19, 66, 115, 118

## W

wages, 14, 24, 135
World War II, 115, 165